The 'Other' in Ourselves

Increasingly, scholars from many disciplines have begun to incorporate various modalities from the humanities and arts – novels, films, artwork, and other forms of expression – to help connect students with the experience of aging in deeply meaningful and person-centered ways. This collection examines how these approaches are incorporated into gerontology and geriatrics education. Rather than focusing solely on measurable outcomes, such as changes in learning over time – which is the purview of empirical pedagogy – chapters focus on strategies for successfully incorporating a specific work into the classroom, descriptions of humanities and/or arts exercises with students or older adults, and other ways that explore how the humanities and arts can be applied successfully and meaningfully in educational settings.

This book was originally published as a special issue of *Geronotology & Geriatrics Education*.

Kate de Medeiros is Associate Professor of Gerontology at Miami University, Oxford, OH, USA. Her research involves narratives in later life and creative expression among people with dementia. She is author of *The Short Guide to Aging and Gerontology* (2016) and *Narrative Gerontology in Research and Practice* (2013), as well as numerous peer-reviewed articles.

Kelly Niles-Yokum is Associate Professor of Gerontology, and the Program Director for the MS in Gerontology, at the University of La Verne, California, USA. Her work focuses on street-level bureaucracy, control and choice in care for the elderly, rural aging and family caregiving. She is the author of *The Aging Networks: A Guide to Programs and Service* (with Wagner, 7th ed., 2010).

Judith L. Howe is Professor in the Brookdale Department of Geriatrics and Palliative Medicine at the Icahn School of Medicine at Mount Sinai, NY, USA. Her career interests include gerontology and geriatric education, interprofessional teamwork, community-based services, geriatric workforce issues and rural health issues. She is the author of *Geriatric Mental Health Disaster and Emergency Preparedness* (with Toner and Miersaw, 2010).

The 'Other' in Ourselves
Exploring the Educational Power of the Humanities and Arts

Edited by
Kate de Medeiros, Kelly Niles-Yokum and Judith L. Howe

LONDON AND NEW YORK

First published 2018 by Routledge

2 Park Square, Milton Park, Abingdon, Oxfordshire OX14 4RN
52 Vanderbilt Avenue, New York, NY 10017

Routledge is an imprint of the Taylor & Francis Group, an informa business

First issued in paperback 2019

Copyright © 2018 Taylor & Francis

All rights reserved. No part of this book may be reprinted or reproduced or utilised in any form or by any electronic, mechanical, or other means, now known or hereafter invented, including photocopying and recording, or in any information storage or retrieval system, without permission in writing from the publishers.

Notice:
Product or corporate names may be trademarks or registered trademarks, and are used only for identification and explanation without intent to infringe.

British Library Cataloguing in Publication Data
A catalogue record for this book is available from the British Library

ISBN 13: 978-1-138-10313-9 (hbk)
ISBN 13: 978-0-367-89107-7 (pbk)

Typeset in ITC Garamond Std
by RefineCatch Limited, Bungay, Suffolk

Publisher's Note
The publisher accepts responsibility for any inconsistencies that may have arisen during the conversion of this book from journal articles to book chapters, namely the possible inclusion of journal terminology.

Disclaimer
Every effort has been made to contact copyright holders for their permission to reprint material in this book. The publishers would be grateful to hear from any copyright holder who is not here acknowledged and will undertake to rectify any errors or omissions in future editions of this book.

Contents

Citation Information vii
Notes on Contributors ix

Introduction – The "Other" in Ourselves: Exploring the Educational
Power of the Humanities and Arts 1
Kate de Medeiros

1. Kate's Journey: Introducing Students to the Human Side of
   Aging Services and Supports 4
   Pamela Pitman Brown and Kelly Niles-Yokum

2. Teaching Through Remembering: Using Written Reminiscences
   in Courses for Older Adults 27
   Elena Bendien

3. Aging and the Arts Online: Lessons Learned From Course
   Development and Implementation 45
   Jacqueline Eaton

4. Transformative Theatre: A Promising Educational Tool for
   Improving Health Encounters With LGBT Older Adults 64
   *Anne K. Hughes, Clare Luz, Dennis Hall, Penny Gardner,
   Chris Walker Hennessey, and Lynn Lammers*

5. Ageing, Drama, and Creativity: Translating Research Into Practice 79
   Jackie Reynolds, Miriam Bernard, Jill Rezzano, and Michelle Rickett

Index 101

Citation Information

The chapters in this book were originally published in *Gerontology & Geriatrics Education*, volume 37, issue 3 (2016). When citing this material, please use the original page numbering for each article, as follows:

Foreword
The "Other" in Ourselves: Exploring the Educational Power of the Humanities and Arts
Kate de Medeiros
Gerontology & Geriatrics Education, volume 37, issue 3 (2016), pp. 229–231

Chapter 1
Kate's Journey: Introducing Students to the Human Side of Aging Services and Supports
Pamela Pitman Brown and Kelly Niles-Yokum
Gerontology & Geriatrics Education, volume 37, issue 3 (2016), pp. 232–254

Chapter 2
Teaching Through Remembering: Using Written Reminiscences in Courses for Older Adults
Elena Bendien
Gerontology & Geriatrics Education, volume 37, issue 3 (2016), pp. 255–272

Chapter 3
Aging and the Arts Online: Lessons Learned From Course Development and Implementation
Jacqueline Eaton
Gerontology & Geriatrics Education, volume 37, issue 3 (2016), pp. 273–291

Chapter 4
Transformative Theatre: A Promising Educational Tool for Improving Health Encounters With LGBT Older Adults
Anne K. Hughes, Clare Luz, Dennis Hall, Penny Gardner, Chris Walker Hennessey, and Lynn Lammers
Gerontology & Geriatrics Education, volume 37, issue 3 (2016), pp. 292–306

CITATION INFORMATION

Chapter 5
Ageing, Drama, and Creativity: Translating Research Into Practice
Jackie Reynolds, Miriam Bernard, Jill Rezzano, and Michelle Rickett
Gerontology & Geriatrics Education, volume 37, issue 3 (2016), pp. 307–328

For any permission-related enquiries please visit:
http://www.tandfonline.com/page/help/permissions

Notes on Contributors

Elena Bendien is a Researcher at University of Humanistic Studies, Utrecht, the Netherlands.

Miriam Bernard is based at the Faculty of Humanities and Social Sciences, Claus Moser Research Centre, Keele University, UK.

Pamela Pitman Brown is Gerontology Program Coordinator and Assistant Professor at the Department of Behavioral Sciences, Winston-Salem State University, USA.

Kate de Medeiros is Associate Professor of Gerontology at Miami University, Oxford, OH, USA.

Jacqueline Eaton is Project Director at the Hartford Center of Geriatric Nursing Excellence, College of Nursing, University of Utah, USA.

Penny Gardner is Assistant Professor of Writing, Rhetoric, and American Culture (WRAC), Michigan State University, USA.

Dennis Hall is based in Lansing, Michigan, USA.

Chris Walker Hennessey is based at the Mental Health Aging Project, Lansing Community College, Lansing, USA.

Judith L. Howe is Professor in the Brookdale Department of Geriatrics and Palliative Medicine at the Icahn School of Medicine at Mount Sinai, NY, USA.

Anne K. Hughes is Associate Professor at the School of Social Work, Michigan State University, USA.

Lynn Lammers is Artistic Coordinator of the Transforming Theatre Ensemble, Michigan State University, USA.

Clare Luz is a tenure track assistant professor in the College of Human Medicine, Michigan State University, USA.

Kelly Niles-Yokum is Associate Professor of Gerontology, and the Program Director for the MS in Gerontology, at the University of La Verne, California, USA.

Jackie Reynolds is Research Associate at the Faculty of Humanities and Social Sciences, Claus Moser Research Centre, Keele University, UK.

NOTES ON CONTRIBUTORS

Jill Rezzano is based at the Faculty of Humanities and Social Sciences, Claus Moser Research Centre, Keele University, UK.

Michelle Rickett is a Research Associate at the Faculty of Humanities and Social Sciences, Claus Moser Research Centre, Keele University, UK.

INTRODUCTION

The "Other" in Ourselves: Exploring the Educational Power of the Humanities and Arts

Long before age was something to be "studied," before statistics, theories, models, hypotheses, longitudinal designs and other empirical approaches became the dominant way knowing, there were the humanities and arts. In ancient Greece, the humanities formed the *"trivium"* (grammar, rhetoric and logic) which, along with the "quadrivium" (artithmetic, geometry, astronomy and music) comprised the ideal education. While the humanities and arts have always included topics and issues involving later life—Shakespeare's *King Lear* which warns of the dangers of surrendering property and care to one's children, the myth of Bacchus and Philamon which extols the virtues of long-standing love and generosity, Rembrandt's self portraits in later life, and countless others—they hold a marginalized place within gerontology and geriatrics. Many textbooks do not mention the important influence of humanities and arts scholarship in the development of the field or provide tools for educators and researchers to include the humanities and arts in their work. This special issue was therefore developed to provide a space for those whose work in the humanities and arts transforms gerontological and geriatric education.

The goal of the humanities and arts has been described as "dedicated to understanding human experience through the disciplined development of insight, perspective, critical understanding, discernment, and creativity" (Cole, Carlin, & Carson, 2014, p. 3). Through cultural representations (e.g., texts, drama, paintings), we can see ourselves through the symbols and stories of others. These cultural representations provide a space for critical reflection and new imagination, to step into places, people and situations that otherwise wouldn't be possible in the physical world. As such, the humanities and arts offer great potential in education, as the articles in this issue demonstrate.

Pamela Pitman Brown and Kelly Niles-Yokum's article describes the use of the novel, *Kate Quinton's Days* by Susan Sheehan in an undergraduate and graduate class. The purpose of the novel was to help students connect to the lives that are affected by long-term care systems, to include the immigrant women working as direct care providers, the daughters of the main character who found their childhood struggles with place and identity within the family resurfaced in the context of caring for their mother, and of course, the main character, Kate Quinton, through flashbacks and reminiscence. The authors note that "the students were able to read and analyze how a family attempts to navigate the complex landscape of care and caring, age and aging, and how, in the end, as they consider their own future selves and career choices, they might be able to make difference as gerontologists, social workers, and advocates for older adults and their families" (p. 248).

Elena Bendien's article focuses on educational courses for older adults themselves using written reminiscence. She writes that "each course that is directed toward a deeper understanding of human life, or—as in our case—of the remembering process and human aging, will benefit from teaching methods with a narrative orientation" (pp. 255–256). The purpose of the narrative approach was to connect the learner with his or her own experiences, which, as the analysis of the writings demonstrated, occurred in a powerful, transformative way.

Jacqueline Eaton's article describes the development of an online course in Aging and the Arts for undergraduate and graduate students. Initially targeted to address the humanities and aging competency developed by AGHE, the course brings in various aspects of aging to explore late life potential through the arts. Students gathered and shared resources associated with aging and the arts, provided links to aging theory and issues, and engaged in discussions and other postings to better understand themselves and their views on aging. As Eaton writes, "The humanities and arts promote a holistic view that moves beyond the deficit model of aging while promoting interdisciplinary collaboration that bridges science and art" (p. 273).

The final two articles describe ways in which theater was used in community settings. The article by Anne K. Hughes and colleagues describes a transformative theatre approach which engaged community activists and academic and community leaders to think deeply and share their thoughts and experiences about the invisibility of older adults within the LGBT community. From this work came a draft script, which, after revisions based on input from the group, was performed for an audience who was asked to provide feedback. This use of art as an integrative form of education, expression, protest, and resolution highlights the potential of the arts to move people in ways that may not be possible through pamphlets, research articles, or other more traditional approaches. As the authors state, "Whether bias is overt, covert, or even unconscious, theatrical frameworks offer the opportunity to observe human behavior; peel back the layers of defensiveness, rationalization, fear, and guardedness within each of the characters; and to ultimately see their humanity. The theatre experience can engender empathy and create a space in which to imagine new behavior, practice, and policy" (p. 294).

While Jackie Reynolds and colleagues also used drama, they did so in a somewhat different way than Hughes et al. The Aging, Drama and Creativity course they describe brought together 18 participants (selected from an applicant pool of 59) for "participatory drama" or active story telling centered around various experiences of aging such as ageism, generational attitudes, myths and stereotypes about aging, and others. Overall, through feedback from participants, they found that "the approach to active learning, the opportunities for reflection on one's own attitudes and experiences of aging, and the emphasis on gaining ideas and tools to be applied in people's practice" (p. 325) were are important, valuable aspects of the course.

Overall, the articles point to the many ways in which tools from the humanities and arts can help students, community members, older persons, gerontologists and so on discover the "other" in themselves. Aging becomes more than a number, a quality, a characteristic, a measurement, and instead is something real that others can experience in some meaningful way. As gerontology and geriatrics continue to move forward, it's important to keep in mind that the questions about aging need not be limited to "how" or "why," but rather should be open to explorations about what it means to grow old.

Kate de Medeiros

REFERENCE

Cole, T. R., Carlin, N. S., & Carson, R. A. (2014). *Medical humanities: An introduction.* Cambridge, UK: Cambridge University Press.

Kate's Journey: Introducing Students to the Human Side of Aging Services and Supports

PAMELA PITMAN BROWN

KELLY NILES-YOKUM

Although using novels to teach aging is not a new concept, teaching the human side of long-term services and supports from the perspective of the care recipient via novels has not been thoroughly explored. Literature often reflects societal norms and issues; thus, the use of a novel in the classroom allows for critical reflection and analysis of self and other, particularly when engaging students in aging concepts and experiences of growing old. This article describes the employment of Kate Quinton's Days *(1984), a novel that brings into focus the important, and often forgotten, human side of aging services and supports. Additionally, the novel focuses on administrative and medical bureaucracy within the context of home health, and family dynamics that come into play with issues of aging and long-term care. Students may have had limited exposure to various aspects of aging and care that play out in the novel, and bringing the character Kate and her life story into the classroom allows for discussions that would not otherwise be as meaningful or instructive. The authors found that students related in important ways to Kate and went beyond the "system" to consider the lived experience of care and support as we age.*

INTRODUCTION

Many of us might recall reading novels in our high school and college courses, particularly novels as part of the curriculum. Novels can convey complex concepts and themes often outside of our realm of life experiences. For example, during a reading of J.D. Salinger's *Catcher in the Rye* (1951), students will encounter themes such as loneliness and isolation, friendship, and loss, all without leaving the comfort of their chair or their own life. Whether students will walk with you across that bridge—using the novel as a way to connect the student to the overall topic, in our case, long-term services and supports—is contingent upon a variety of factors including the topic at hand, how the material is presented, and whether the instructor has provided sufficient background and context in terms of how, what, and why.

Novels incorporate reality into a narrative, allowing a stop and restart, to gain more information or background. Using novels in the classroom can cultivate critical thinking, interpretation, and analytic skills necessary for navigating the real world, outside of the classroom, and allow students to collaborate with other students and the professor, and explore various interpretations or analyses, which they may not have considered. Literature often reflects societal norms and issues, thus, the use of a novel in the classroom allows for critical reflection and analysis of self and other, particularly when engaging students in aging concepts and experiences of growing old. Additionally, some novels may provide the student with glimpses into a world that they are about to enter, such as their chosen profession. As the humanities seek to integrate aging material into their coursework (Port & Swinnen, 2014), gerontologists are seeking new ways of integrating humanities into their pedagogical repertoire as well.

Teaching aging via novels is not a new concept, but utilizing a novel to demonstrate the human side of long-term services and supports from the perspective of the care recipient lacks prior description. This article describes the use of *Kate Quinton's Days* (Sheehan, 1984), as an experimental pedagogical approach, using a novel that brings into focus the human side of long-term services and supports. Additionally, the novel focuses on administrative and medical bureaucracy within the context of home health, and family dynamics, which are on display via Kate and her children, such as concern over long-term care and caregiving expectations. Gerontology students, particularly those who are undergraduate and traditional age, may have had limited exposure to various aspects of aging and care portrayed in the novel. Graduate students come to the topic of aging from a variety of perspectives and may already be working in the field or caring for their own family member. Whatever the background and the age of the student a novel such as this can be the bridge that brings everyone on the journey together around the topic.

Two gerontologists came together to discuss an exploratory pedagogical tool using the novel *Kate Quinton's Days*, with students at two different universities. We were interested in the following: how would students react to a novel in class, and could the novel be a useful way of getting students to connect to the material. The purpose of this assignment was an exploration on utilizing a novel such as this in our gerontology classrooms. This article describes the instructor's impressions of our students' engagement with the novel. We went in not knowing what to expect and, most importantly, not having any expectations.

Review of the Literature: The Importance of Integrating Humanities and Arts Into Gerontology and Geriatrics

Sheets (2013) notes, "Integrating novels into our (gerontology) courses can help students link the objective content of aging with the subjective human aspects" (p. 1061). Zeilig (1997) notes the importance of integrating humanities into gerontology and geriatrics, referencing Kohl (1988, p. 368), who suggests we not segment applied or scientific fields from the humanity, and that we should work together when dealing with or discussing/examining aging. Zeilig (1997) notes that Cole and colleagues (1992, p. 8) state the humanities are relevant to aging because "we are asked to contemplate not only a proposition but the proposer ... we hear the human voice behind what is said" (Oró, 2009, p. 39).

Many compelling reasons exist to integrate humanities and arts into gerontology and geriatrics including consideration of ethical dilemmas and related insight into human nature intrinsic within the humanities discipline. Additionally, the integration allows for blurring the lines between the character in the story, and the students themselves, thereby giving students permission to question whether they, if placed in the character's position, would chose the same options, have similar or different feelings, and perhaps even contemplate their own reality within the character's situational context. Nussbaum (1998) suggests that novels develop "moral capacities without which citizens will not succeed in making reality out of the normative conclusion of any moral or political theory, however excellent" (p. 364). Developing moral capacities in gerontology and geriatrics is paramount as students go forward and will work with persons who may have limited abilities and/or capacity for consent. West (1993) writes, "Literature helps us understand others ... helps us sympathize with their pain, it helps us share their sorrow, and it helps us celebrate their joy. It makes us more moral. It makes us better people" (p. 263). West (2015) later states that knowledge acquired through literature is a "peculiar sort of knowledge" that "moves us rather than informs us," and that knowledge of the other(s) acquired through this medium, "becomes a part of our sense of self, our sense of the other, and our sense of union with him" (p. 133).

An additional reason to integrate humanities and arts into gerontology and geriatric education is to provide an opportunity for students to view life in a more realistic way and view the aging experience through a literary lens. Posner (1997) noted,

> The rise of the novel coincided with the rise of the bourgeoisie, the expansion of literacy, and the growth of science and philosophical realism-developments that stimulated demand for a form of literature that would depict realistically the activities and experiences of ordinary life. (p. 6)

Posner's statement allows literary construction based on a realistic, ordinary, unremarkable life, someone similar to Kate. Additionally, Waxman (2005) notes that literature is "an important cultural artifact" (p. 78), which contributes to one's beliefs, attitudes, and values concerning aging. It is through the stories of older adults, where students can begin to visualize attitudes toward older adult, and critically analyze if these attitudes are ageist or not. Similarly, Burke (1989) posits the concept that "reading is a form of doing" (Waxman, 2005, p. 78) whereby reading about the aging experience or processes is a way of trying on aging prior to the actual elder experience.

An additional benefit of using realistic life and viewing the aging experience through a literary lens includes opportunities to explore intergenerational relationships and potentially promote positive change toward older adults. The use of literature in place of physical intergenerational relationship in the current family climate, where there may exist spatial segregation or distance from their older relatives, may suffice in the promotion of positive change/understanding (Jarrott & McCann, 2013). Jarrott and McCann's (2013) conclusions indicate that characters within the chosen literature did move toward positive change but stressed the fact that "fantastical representations may wield less influence on readers' ideas because the situations may not translate to everyday experiences" (p. 303). Their research strengthens using literature to convey empathy, understanding, and create positive change toward older adults, strengthening the concept of using an unremarkable, ordinary character such as Kate.

Utilization of the humanities and arts to assist in the portrayal of gerontological theories is yet another reason to integrate literature into a course. Karasik and colleagues (2014) discuss the use of films to explore theories or key concepts of an aging curriculum. Toman (2008) notes this premise, utilizing novels or fiction within social science or professional disciplines, to "embody abstract concepts so that students may approach an idea both deductively as a statement to be applied to the world and inductively as a case study in search of an organizing principle" (p. 194). Rubin (1990) found portrayal of older adults within literature to illuminate the social and personal concerns of aging. Rosenblatt (1983) posits the cultural function of literature is one as an agent to "transmit images of behavior, emotional attitudes… and social and personal standards" (p. 223; cited in Waxman, 2005, p. 78).

Review of the Literature: The Use of Novels as a Pedagogical Tool in the Gerontology Classroom

Moss (1978) suggests that "Humanists and the humanities can help the public to perceive that aging and old age can be richer experiences than they presently are in the United States" (p. 581). Bringing depth and meaning to aging and old age is challenging within a classroom environment, but it provides an opportunity, that if structured and well thought out, can bring students to a place of engagement, empathy, and energize them about aging.

Novels, as a pedagogical tool within the classroom, humanize older adults in a way that other approaches cannot. Tice, Harnek Hall, and Miller (2010) note that using literature as a classroom tool to mediate stereotypes and tear down the walls of the us and them mentality is a powerful approach that is sustainable beyond the classroom. "The process of reading about the lives of older adults can give students insight into a different life stage…. Reflecting upon literature provides students opportunities to explore a population against which they may have biases," (Tice et al., 2010, p. 721). Gattuso and Saw (1998) agree, finding that students reported an "enhanced awareness of stereotyping" (p. 279) and that the narratives provided a framework for discussing a variety of topics related to aging and old age.

Many gerontological scholars have written about attitudes and aging, and some have suggested transformation of students' negative attitudes concerning aging can occur if they "learn to associate their own experiences in personal growth with parallel experiences in the growth of the elderly" (Wolf, 1987, p. 289). Further, Morgan (2012) suggests that students come to gerontology with their own worldviews, their own perspectives or paradigms that have helped to construct their own views of old age and aging. The humanities provides students an opportunity to explore not only their current paradigm but also their existing attitudes about aging, their origins, and the impact this personal aging ethos can have on our personal, work, and relational lives. Incorporating narrative literature on aging into the course curriculum, implemented in a thoughtful and meaningful way, can deepen and broaden one's understanding of old age and aging.

Documentation exists in support of the use of literature as a pedagogical tool, particularly the use of literature as a model in the classroom to address issues related to attitudes and stereotypes. Black and Miranda (2008) discuss the use of novels within social work practice courses. They note that novels are also useful at the personal level to address one's own personal biases and to encourage self-awareness and self-understanding, a paramount skill needed when working with diverse populations. It is this vicarious tour while reading a novel, whether fiction or nonfiction, that allows for self-awareness, self-criticism, and self-understanding. However, to be effective an incorporation of supplemental methods must accompany the primary material, allowing students to examine critically what they are reading, thinking, and feeling, and then to apply it in ways that provide an outlet for discussions and dialogue.

Wolf (1987) proposes a dual perspective to gerontological education that includes providing information about the norm of aging, that it is a universal experience, and secondly, that aging is a stage that we can all identify with regardless of our own age or where we are in the process at any time (p. 289). Our role as educators is to seek to provide a foundation of learning and facilitate a deeper analysis of the content and ensure a meaningful place for discussions.

Studies indicate that novels and narratives also motivate and assist readers in their comprehension of a subject, particularly a subject with which they may have little to no exposure or experience. Other studies indicate opportunities for critical thinking and analysis as well as an alternative to a traditional textbook (Clark, 2013; Gorman, 2003; Schwarz, 2006). Not only is a novel or narrative a motivation for students but it also allows for creative and innovative interaction with the instructor. The instructor can bring an excitement into the classroom and, along with the students, delight in the discovery of a new element that may have previously gone unnoticed, for example. It also allows the instructor to show the relevance of gerontology or geriatrics in a realistic setting, one that is not classic textbook, and not contrived.

Rosenblatt (1995) discusses how literature is often a spectator sport, where one sits on the sidelines and does not participate in the analysis, and not from a personal perspective. She also notes that students should be able or allowed to approach the literature from the personal perspective, where the literary work has meaning, personal meaning to the student, and the student's response to the novel should be encouraged, and is worth expressing. In other words, the importance of using the novel via the students' expressions of their reaction to the text should be encouraged and should not necessarily be limited to a carefully structured analysis via the instructor.

Description of Sheehan's Novel, *Kate Quinton's Days*

Kate Quinton's Days (*KQD*) (Sheehan, 1984) chronicles one year in the life of 80-year-old Kate Quinton. Sheehan follows Kate from February 24, 1982 to February 24, 1983. Kate is described as a "pale, thin elderly woman" (p. 1), and our first introduction to her is when she is in a hospital bed in Brooklyn's Lutheran Medical Center. It is within the first few pages that we learn Kate's admission date as well as her chief medical complaint, and Sheehan introduces Kate's numerous doctors and prior ailments. Also introduced is

Claire Quinton, one of Kate's daughters, who is currently her primary caregiver. Using Kate's intake form at the hospital we learn that Kate was born on February 11, 1902 in Scotland, she is Catholic and attends Immaculate Heart of Mary Catholic Church. We also learn the basis of Kate's Medicare and Social Security benefits comes from her husband's work history, as she draws widow's benefits. These elements not only set the stage for the reader getting to know the main character, but also provide a strong foundation for classroom discussions and related issues related to long-term-care provision and access, financial issues, family dynamics, and importantly, Kate's life course experiences as they relate to her life and old age.

Throughout the book, Sheehan goes into great detail concerning Medicare, Medicaid/Medicaid eligibility or dual eligibility, home health care, comorbid conditions of older adults, the bureaucracy of governmental assistance/ entitlement programs, as well as the demographic elements of Brooklyn and the home health industry. She brings a focus on the working conditions of home health aides, and the transitory patterns that still plague the industry, as Kate had 15 home attendants during the year. A discussion of the health of her primary caregiver, Claire, allows emphasis on how the health of a caregiver can substantially alter the course of treatments or living accommodations of the older adult.

Although Sheehan does not address the issue of burden of care, or effect of parent care, there are signs noted in Claire's health, and challenging emotional strain, of the level of the care that she is providing to Kate. Brody (2004) notes those women who have fewer competing responsibilities, and those who are not married, often provide caregiving to the parent (p. 99). In addition, there is more of an expectation for that daughter to move in with the elderly parent (p. 99). Brody (2004) notes that married daughters provided less help to the elderly parent(s) than the nonmarried one (Lang & Brody, 1983).

Sheehan also delves into the complexities of family relationships. She particularly focuses on the strain of continued sibling rivalry between Kate's daughters, Barbara and Claire, often bringing the conflict to the reader's attention through the retelling of past life events. With a classic case of favored child/rejected child, the retelling of the past events only strengthens Brody's (2004) discoveries, where the "rejected child" may wholly care for the elderly parent, hoping to gain the status as "favored child" (p. 101). It is this level of detail within the narrative that marks *KQD* as a capacious gerontology classroom pedagogical tool.

The structure of *KQD* is not a memoir formatting oft used for older adults' life stories. De Medeiros (2007) notes that various literary forms may not include information needed for the reader to make sense of the story such as a letter to a friend. One can leave out background information because the friend already knows the background, or the writer deems it unimportant. With Sheehan writing *KQD* in the third-person narrative, more in-depth information provides the reader an ability to comprehend Kate's life story.

Pedagogical Approach

PROCESS AND USE OF *KATE QUINTON'S DAYS* IN THE CLASSROOM

KQD was used as a pedagogical tool in our gerontology courses which included one undergraduate (Instructor 1) and one graduate course (Instructor 2), specifically as a portion of the course content focused on the human side of aging services and supports. As a classroom exercise, we received an exempt review approval from our respective Institutional Review Boards. Both authors approached their Institutional Review Office and received Exempt Review status per Federal Regulation 45CFR46. The need for consent was waived, as students were not identifiable within the redacted classroom material.

KQD is a novel that focuses on the administrative and medical bureaucracy within the context of home health and long-term care. This provides a different platform than a textbook in that it helps to bring to life the characters addressing and living the issues themselves. *KQD* may also be a tool to address family dynamics, which come into play with families who are involved in the complexities of family caregiving including issues related to addressing an older adult's needs as well as other generational or relationship needs, such as children or spouses/partners.

KQD is eight chapters and 158 pages of text, allowing the student the ability to consume the novel in about an 8-week time frame, particularly if using more analytical tools such as mappings events and characters, or reading for content specific information. Instructor 1 utilized *KQD* for a shorter time frame with graduate students during a 6-week summer course. Additionally, Instructor 1 found the novel works well in a traditional semester course as part of regular course content. The students read two to three chapters a week of the novel, along with aging/health supplemental readings, and mapping of characters/health challenges. The final class project consisted of a paper concentrating on the health challenges of a chosen character from the book. Instructor 2 used the novel during a 10-week term course and found the novel worked well within that time frame.

STUDENT REACTIONS TO USING A NOVEL IN THE CLASSROOM

One of our pedagogical concerns was how students would react to using a novel, either instead of a textbook or as a supplemental book, in class. An answer was established rather quickly, for as soon as it was mentioned within the first day, some of the undergraduate students began to cheer, whereas others immediately began to criticize the approach. Undergraduate and graduate students alike are generally accustomed to using a traditional textbook. Stepping outside of the traditional classroom concept takes students into the unknown and may make them uncomfortable. We found that one way to address this was to assure students, who may be concerned with fully comprehending the novel as it related to the objectives of the course, that we would be working together as a group for this project. Additionally, the students received assurance that connections to the course objectives would in a variety of ways, vis-à-vis course assignments related to the project, which included character and event mapping, reading aloud, and reflective writing, assist them.

There were benefits and drawbacks on using a novel, which was more than 30 years old. One benefit was a low purchase price. Each instructor purchased several copies and "loaned" them to the students. Additionally, each instructor placed copies in the reserved section of the library for students' use. One drawback was the current use of gerontology/geriatric service terminology versus the 1980s use of senior service terminology. Instructors found that the difference in terminology allowed for stimulating discussions related to generational differences, including how important language is, as it can shape our attitudes and perpetuate ageist attitudes and norms, but perhaps more importantly, how numerous phenomena within the system have remained unchanged.

Classroom Use of Novel

A preliminary use of *KQD* occurred in the spring of 2014 for Instructor 1, as an alternative activity for a theory to practice course. A modification of a spring 2015 theory to practice course included required usage of *KQD*. The structure of the course made allowance for a review of gerontological theories during the first 3 weeks, with the reading of *KQD* beginning in Week 4. An additional allowance was given to students who were simultaneously enrolled in the course "Legal, Political, and Economic Aspects of Aging," whereby an expansion of the final paper component could include *KDQ*.

Instructor 2 brought the novel in to a graduate level gerontology course titled "Managing Services for Older Adults." Introduction of the novel occurred on the first night of class, and the instructor provided background and instructions. The novel was an additional assignment and included chapter-by-chapter reading and reflection followed by discussions at each class session, led by individual students.

Students and Settings

We worked with two groups of students, one undergraduate class (Instructor 1), and one graduate class (Instructor 2). The instructors were working together in the spring of 2015 at different institution in different states. Our goals in using *KQD* were as follows:

1. integrating the novel into the class;
2. introduce students to a personal story of an older adult and her family;

3. show the complexities of a family's navigation of trials/tribulations of long-term-care services and supports;
4. present the human side of aging services and supports; and
5. and work together as educators in different settings, understanding our approaches and learning from one another as we went.

Undergraduate Class

The university representing the undergraduate students is a public research, coeducational, Historically Black College and University (HBCU). The gerontology program at the University is currently an Association of Gerontology in Higher Education (AGHE) Program of Merit, with a bachelors of arts in gerontology degree and gerontology minor. The student enrollment is 5,200, with a student to faculty ratio of 18:1. The University accommodates students' diverse backgrounds and provides multiple entry points in order to accommodate life situations, diverse socioeconomic levels, and the nontraditional student. The University demographic population is approximately 74% African American, and approximately 60% female. Traditional students (age 18–22) are approximately 51% of the population, which gives classes a wider variety of age groupings. The University supports pedagogical formats, which are identified as "high impact practices" (Winston-Salem State University Strategic Planning Commission, 2010, p. 12) focusing on liberal arts learning outcomes, and application of classroom learning to the outside world.

The 11 female students participating in the project were a blend of traditional/nontraditional students, with a majority of African American students, and a majority of nontraditional students older than age 25. As the course is required of all gerontology majors, the students were either undergraduate gerontology majors/minors or Interdisciplinary students with a gerontology focus/concentration.

Graduate Class

The University representing the graduate class is a private nonprofit university in California identified as a Hispanic Serving Institution. Total enrollment is 8,517 including adult learners, graduate, law, and online students. The main campus includes approximately 2,713 traditional undergraduates and approximately 2,863 main campus graduate, doctoral, and law students. Student to faculty ratio is 14:1 and two thirds of classes have fewer than 20 students. Students that participated in this project were students in a masters in gerontology program at the university. The three students selected for this experience were enrolled in a directed study course titled "Managing Aging Services." Students included a diverse group of students. This class was selected specifically due to the focus of the course where the novel *KQD* could be used as a tool to explore issues related to managing aging services.

Specific Exercises: *Kate Quinton's Days*

UNDERGRADUATE CLASS

A review of gerontological theories took place during the first 3 weeks of the theory to practice course for Instructor 1. The class began Week 4 by reading the novel aloud and numerous students found this to be uncomfortable at first, as evidenced by comments such as, "I don't want to read out loud" and "I don't feel comfortable doing this," "are you serious?" After realizing that some of the characters' unfamiliar and ethnically diverse names were difficult for students to pronounce and everyone was struggling, we were able to have a productive discussion about how important it was to, in fact, read together as a class. Reading the book aloud for the second 4 weeks of the course provides students with an opportunity to invest in the story and may allow for deeper engagement of the gerontological content with their peers vis-à-vis direct interaction and sense of community that reading aloud provides (Rasinski, 2003). Additionally, reading aloud together (RAT) allows the student to analyze the content through a gerontological lens and discuss gerontological theoretical constructs or theories with others in their field. This pedagogical approach is appropriate, where literature likewise illustrates theories and constructs within other disciplines (Clowers & Mori, 1977; Coser, 1972; Hall, 2000; Hendershott & Wright, 1993; Sullivan, 1982).

RAT, with a book in hand, provides differentiating learning processes for visual and auditory learners. Benefits of RAT include fluency. When people read aloud and practice reading aloud repeatedly, they are increasing their fluency levels significantly (Rasinski & Padak, 2000). RAT also increases comprehension, through prosodic or expressive reading of the text (Apol & Harris, 1999; Paige, Rasinski, & Magpuri-Lavell, 2012). RAT also enhances/develops reading skills such as critical reading/listening, as well as memory, attention, and sequencing (Healy, 1990). Students will understand collaborative learning as they come together to read, and receive feedback from others, as well as an exchange of ideas and confidence building. Struggling readers will become stronger readers through listening to others read, and they can become more fluid and confident readers (Armbruster, Lehr, & Osborn, 2001). It also produces a community of support and encouragement (Egan, 1991; Rasinski, 2003).

In the undergraduate class, RAT allowed the instructor to better answer questions or discussions on characters, policies, or dyadic/triadic relationships within the story in real-time. RAT allowed the class to read, stop, discuss, question, and then move forward in the reading, with the possibility of returning to an earlier conversation or paragraph. Additionally, RAT allowed the instructor to review the character/event mapping worksheets with the students in real-time, as well as assist students during the class time in understanding the mapping, and reasons behind it.

The initial conception and subsequent reading of *KQD* indicated a need to keep up with the characters and the sequence of events. Numerous times throughout the novel flashbacks of Kate's life occur, which are somewhat germane to the present time, thus character and event mapping was a necessity in following the story line. Character and event mapping is often used within literature courses when there are many entrances/exits of characters, and flashback or reminiscence is used within the novel. High school literature instructors utilize this technique when teaching novels during literature courses (Hutchinson, 1995).

A simple way of keeping track with the characters and events is to create two electronic spreadsheets, one on events, and one on the characters (see Appendix A). For the characters, the students keep up with the chapter/page in which the character enters the story, as well as subsequent entrances, the character's name, their relationship to Kate, their job/position, and the student's impression of the person.

Rosenblatt (1983) discusses the analysis of characters within novels per the student's view simply stating that students will often "pass judgement on the actions of characters they encounter" (p. 17). We found that this occurred with students' character analysis, particularly of those they found mean or hateful. One specific comment in *KQD* the students responded to emotionally was Barbara's comment to Claire, "Get yourself together, Claire. There are three things you have to do. Lose Weight. Get a job. And get someone in to share the expense of the apartment" (Sheehan, 1984, p. 13). Students indicated they were "disappointed" with Barbara's tone and comments. Rosenblatt (1983) also discusses the additional necessary components to understanding and analysis of the characters through the reading of the novel for each individual student:

> The text brings into the reader's consciousness certain concepts, certain sensuous experiences, and certain images of things, people, actions, and scenes. The special meanings and, more particularly, the submerged associations that these words and images have for the individual reader will largely determine what the work communicates to *him*. (p. 30)

Rosenblatt went on to discuss how each individual student brings his or her own personality, past memories, immediate personal needs and concerns, as well to the reading and later the analysis of the work (p. 30).

For the events, the students enter the chapter the event occurred, the date noted within the novel, the page number associated with the event, a description of the event, and the student's impression of the event. Additionally, for the historical fiscal construct of the novel the students logged financial transactions, noting chapter/page, why funds/monies was exchanged, and they were asked to recalculate the funds per current year via an inflation calculator.

The students later use the character and event mappings as well as the financial transactions in class and within the final paper. To facilitate learning, the first week of reading Chapter 1, Week 4 of the course, the class participated in the character/event mappings as a group during class time.

GRADUATE STUDENTS

The graduate students were introduced to *KQD* during the first class as part of their orientation to the course and the term objectives. They were required to have the novel as well as a textbook titled, *Long-term Care: Managing across the Continuum* (Pratt, 2010). Because the novel is easily accessible at prices from .01 to 10.00 via Amazon and other book retailers the instructor bought copies for all students to use.

Students were each required to have a copy of the book and were each assigned a specific chapter where they would lead the class discussion and provide a forum for discussion and analysis. Students submitted reflections weekly, by chapter, via Blackboard Learning Management system. The reflections also served as discussions for our weekly face-to-face meetings. Students were instructed to consider questions on chapter take-away, relate material to class content, changes they would make if they were the administrators, and what was new or surprising to them. Each answer was to be framed around the human side of long-term services and supports, and the criteria from our textbook (Pratt, 2010) (see Appendix B).

The readings from the novel were not only meant to bring the main character, Kate Quinton, into our classroom and provide a face to the many complex issues of care and support, but to also connect students to the rest of the class content, including their main text *Long-term Care: Managing Across the Continuum* (Pratt, 2010). The readings were also to provide the students' connections to the issues related to what our long-term services and supports system should look like in terms of who it serves and how we maintain the focus on the consumer.

In addition to the weekly reflections and discussions students were each responsible for being chapter leaders at various points in the term. The opportunities to lead and facilitate discussions were to empower students in their efforts to become effective leaders on a particular topic or subject. All student developed and submitted an outline for their chapters, with a requirement to connect their chapter to current events and the main textbook.

Student Reflections/Observations

UNDERGRADUATE STUDENTS

Undergraduate students observed with surprise at how the stories and issues were analogous even though 30 years had passed. Students wrote the following:

> Kate was discriminated against within a system put in place to help her. Access to quality care and resources were frequently block or placed on hold by the social worker. The social worker (Ida Winkle) slowed the delivery of service because she believed Kate and her daughter were not deserving of assistance. (Undergraduate student)

> The differences in Kate's social class and her daughter Barbara's social class caused conflict within the family. She (Barbara) tried to manipulate the situation by blaming them for their circumstances. (Undergraduate student)

> The caregivers in this novel were almost all first generation immigrants, or were poor, and were themselves struggling to catch a break and support their families. (Undergraduate student)

Incorporating narrative literature on aging into course curriculum can help to deepen and broaden one's understanding of gerontological theoretical concepts. One student addressed how she viewed Kate through continuity theory's perspective,

> Kate's reaction to the change in her life was expected. According to the continuity theory a person likes to keep their same lifestyle, rituals, morals, and etc. ... from their younger age ... she really had a hard time adapting to the change. Kate loves consistency and didn't mind expressing her feelings on the things on her mind that were changing ... she did not like someone telling her that she could not drink and smoke when she was hospitalized for her poor health. (Undergraduate student)

"Aging successfully" was mentioned by an undergraduate student, who viewed Kate as "aging successfully" even though she was in poor health. She also added a theoretical component of continuity theory, and its applicability, as Kate was "applying familiar patterns and procedures to lessen disruption in her life." The student indicated Kate was aging successfully based on the premise that she was still trying to live as independently as possible and that she "still had some fight left in her."

Only one undergraduate student noted how Kate's housing affected her life stating,

> The apartment has not been remodeled or retrofitted for an elderly individual with numerous complications. Her apartment, like many of those in the New York area, is built with the notion that the resident will be physically fit, and able to climb stairs.

An undergraduate student who works within the field of aging stated that people like Ida Winkel, Kate's case manager, who dealt with Claire on a home-care attendant for Kate through Human Resources Administration, made it difficult for others, within her job and the very people she was supposed to help. The student wrote that, "Ida did not seem happy and appeared bitter towards her clients and co-workers and her job performance reflected it" (Sheehan, 1984, pp. 74–77). During the pages of the novel describing Ida and her method of dealing with her cases/clients, students commented they knew people within the system like Mrs. Winkel. The class erupted into cheers when Claire called Ida's supervisor, reporting her arrogance and verbal abuse (Sheehan, 1984, p. 63). It was clear from the students' comments they were invested, and were involved in both Kate's and Claire's outcome. It was validating, particularly as an instructor, to observe the classroom community created through the reading of *KQD*.

GRADUATE STUDENTS

The graduate students were required to connect the readings from the novel to the textbook material, as a way to integrate the two as a foundation for their writings. Although the reflections were not analyzed for content they were informative and assisted us to see that they had sufficiently grasped the materials presented in class, previous course materials, outside readings, and prior learned gerontological knowledge, including gerontological theoretical concepts in a meaningful way. The novel and related assignments were intended to illustrate the pedagogical tools available to gerontological instructors.

> Mrs. Quinton is definitely in need of long-term care. According to the text, consumers of long-term care are "those persons requiring health-care, personal care, social services, and other supportive services over a sustained period of time" (Pratt). The struggle in this situation is not only about Mrs. Quinton's physical condition and Karen's physical condition. The struggle is also from a financial state they were not able to afford much. Karen wanted the best nursing facility for her mother, however since they were still trying to figure out the Medicaid, Medicare situation it was difficult to find many nursing homes that would cover her costs of living.

> Chapter 2 really surprised me. What surprised me the most in this chapter was Transitional Community Placement, or TCP. After reading chapter 1 I expected that Mrs. Quinton would be placed in a nursing facility. I was very surprised that there was such a program where she can go home and she can be taken care of. TCP was basically her dreams coming true. I was trying to put myself in her daughter's situation. I would definitely rather have my mother come home instead of going to a nursing home however, with five spinal fusions and she can barely walk it must be very difficult for her to take care of her mom.

> Chapter 2 of *Kate Quinton's Days*, really resonated with me for many reasons, but mainly for the lack of care and attention she received.

Previously, I was community liaison at an elder abuse and neglect law firm. While working there, I saw many patients with severe bedsores and who were not treated with adequate care. Kate Quinton suffered through deteriorating health at the hospital, which included swollen feet, back pain, and bedsores, but she was not removed from her bed as often as she should have been. I really felt for Kate throughout this chapter, no one took the time to listen to what she wanted until the T.C.P program was on the table. Her constant longing to go home was never attended to.

Even though *KQD* is from 1984, we hoped what would become a point of analysis and reflection for the graduate and undergraduate students was what if anything has changed within the long-term care system. Students wrote the following,

Doctors and social workers only referred to her daughter, even though Kate was competent and had the ability to answer for herself. (Graduate student)

The author involves the reader and has them feel as if they are present throughout this entire process. I find it refreshing and a true illustration of how the older population is written off in the healthcare system. (Graduate student)

What Kate Quinton is going through is very unfortunate. It must be even more difficult for Claire Quinton who is not only caring for her mother, and trying her best to keep her away from a nursing home, but she is also trying to care for own self at the same time. However, there comes a time when as much as we want to help other family members we need to stop and think and realize that sometimes it's just not doable. (Graduate student)

Limitations and Challenges of Using *KQD* as a Pedagogical Exercise

Although Sheehan's novel covers a year in the life of Kate, portions take on the memoir format. We learn about Kate's younger years in Scotland, her family background in immigration, as well as health information per reminiscence.

One noted limitation was the difference in the final student papers of those who had and who had not worked within the aging network/aging facilities in final papers of the students. Those who had worked within the aging/network or with older adults incorporated some personal past work experiences within their final papers. There were vast differences between nontraditional and traditional students within the utilization of past experience to relate to a new understanding or a more complex understanding of the material, at the undergraduate and graduate level. Rosenblatt (1983, p. 26) acknowledges the differences between the traditional student and the older student, instructing the teacher to assist in the meaning making of the text by beginning at the individualistic starting point of their knowledge acquisition and growth.

Another noted limitation with the undergraduate students was the intensity of the writing and research into their chosen topic. Not all students enter a classroom with the same skills and background. This led to a restructuring of the course, where for the last 3 weeks the class relocated to a writing lab and an allocation of class time focused on research and writing. The instructor was available to assist the student with additional research skill building and assist with draft review/revisions.

DISCUSSION AND CONCLUSION

The overall purpose of this article was to describe the use of the novel as a pedagogical tool in gerontology classes. Integrating the novel *Kate Quinton's Days* (Sheehan, 1984) into gerontology classes provided an opportunity introduce the human side of aging into issues related to aging services and supports on two different campuses. No formal evaluation of the students' engagement or knowledge was conducted, and thus, this article reflected the experience and impressions of the two instructors. Although we approached this project in slightly different ways, within both courses students wrote about having an increased understanding of aging and long-term services and supports. The use of a novel like *KQD* allowed us to open up a whole new world of meaning and perspective to our students while keeping them grounded in gerontological experiences in the context of our past and current acute and long-term care systems in the United States. As students got to know Kate and the other characters, they came to know individuals but, more importantly, had exposure to an insider's view of a family. The students were able to read and analyze how a family attempts to navigate the complex landscape of care and caring, age and aging, and how, in the end, as they consider their own future selves and career choices, they might be able to make a difference as gerontologists, social workers, and advocates for older adults and their families.

It is our goal to continue this work and to continue introducing our students to a world of literature that helps them to understand aging in a way that traditional textbooks cannot offer. As was noted earlier, knowledge acquired through literature or narrative is a "peculiar sort of knowledge" that "moves us rather than informs us," and that knowledge of the other or others acquired through this medium, "becomes a part of our sense of self, our sense of the other, and our sense of union with him" (West, 2015, p. 133). Although in class we might have a discussion on caregiver stress, several students noted this topic running through *KQD*. One in particular stated how Claire, Kate's daughter, gained weight while having her own health issues, and caring for her mother. This highlights the caregiver burden on a caregiver's physical health. She also commented on how family "may become stressed because they are unprepared to bring their loved one home after discharge from a facility."

Waxman (2010) states literature amuses us, but it also brings to the forefront a reflection of "the society in which they are produced" as well as the ability to change and challenge people's "attitudes and politics" as well as affect the world. "Literature can take us out of ourselves and our usual settings, making us more conscious of our own unexamined beliefs and assumptions and giving us new food for thought" (Waxman, 2010, p. 83). As gerontology educators, we should not only inform our students, but also move them and inspire them to work through their own "unexamined beliefs and assumptions." Literature provides a medium that allows us to do this. As previously noted, literature often reflects societal norms and relevant issues. Even the use of an older novel within a classroom allows for critical reflection, as well as the analysis of self and other. Additionally, when attempting to engage students in concepts related to aging and experiences of growing old creativity and innovation may be important as the content itself.

REFERENCES

Apol, L., & Harris, J. (1999). Joyful noises: Creating poems for voices and ears. *Language Arts, 76*(4), 314–322.

Armbruster, B., Lehr, F., & Osborn, J. (2001). *Put reading first: The research building blocks for teaching children to read!* Washington, DC: National Institute for Literacy, National Institute of Child Health and Human Development, U.S. Department of Education.

Black, P., & Miranda, M. M. (2008). The use of contemporary novels as a method of teaching social work micropractice. In C. C. Irvine (Ed.), *Teaching the novel across the curriculum: A handbook for educators* (pp. 299–309). Westwood, CT: Greenwood Press.

Brody, E. M. (2004). *Women in the middle: Their parent care years* (2nd ed.). New York, NY: Springer Publishing.

Burke, K. (1989). Literature as equipment for living. In D. H. Richter (Ed.), *The critical tradition: Classic texts and contemporary trends* (pp. 512–517). New York, NY: St: Martin's Press.

Clark, J. S. (2013). "Your credibility could be shot"; Preservice teachers' thinking about nonfiction graphic novels, curriculum decision making, and professional acceptance. *Social Studies, 104,* 38–45. doi:10.1080/00377996.2012.665957

Clowers, M. L., & Mori, S. H. (1977). *Understanding sociology through fiction.* New York, NY: McGraw-Hill.

Cole, T., Van Tassel, D., & Kastenbaum, R. (Eds.). (1992). *The handbook of the humanities & ageing.* New York, NY: Springer.

Coser, L. A. (1972). *Sociology through literature.* Englewood Cliffs, NJ: Prentice Hall.

De Medeiros, K. (2007). Beyond the memoir: Telling life stories using multiple literary forms. *Journal of Aging, Humanities, and the Arts, 1*(3), 159–167. doi:10.1080/19325610701638052

Egan, K. (1991). *Imagination in teaching and learning: The middle school years.* Chicago, IL: University of Chicago Press.

Gattuso, S., & Saw, C. (1998). Humanistic education in gerontology—A case study using narrative. *Educational Gerontology, 24*, 279–285.

Gorman, M. (2003). *Getting graphic: Using graphic novels to promote literacy with preteens and teens*. Washington, OH: Linworth.

Hall, K. J. (2000). Putting the pieces together: Using Jane Smiley's "A Thousand Acres" in sociology of families. *Teaching Sociology, 28*(4), 370–378. doi:10.2307/1318586

Healy, J. (1990). *Endangered minds: Why children don't think and what to do about it*. New York, NY: Touchstone Books.

Hendershott, A., & Wright, S. (1993). Bringing the sociological perspective into the interdisciplinary classroom through literature. *Teaching Sociology, 21*(4), 325–331. doi:10.2307/1319081

Hutchinson, L. (1995). *Student maps, character maps. Teaching literature in high school: The novel*. Urbana, IL: National Council of Teachers of English.

Jarrott, S. E., & McCann, B. R. (2013). Analysis of intergenerational relationships in adolescent fiction using a contact theory framework. *Gerontology & Geriatrics Education, 34*(3), 292–308. doi:10.1080/02701960.2012.737387

Karasik, R. J., Hamon, R., Writz, J., & Reddy, A. M. (2014). Two thumbs up: Using popular films in introductory aging courses. *Gerontology & Geriatrics Education, 35*(1), 86–113. doi:10.1080/02701960.2012.749253

Kohl, S. (1988). Ageing as a challenge for sociological theory. *Ageing & Society, 8*, 367–394. doi:10.1017/S0144686X00007169

Lang, A., & Brody, E. M. (1983). Characteristics of middle-aged daughters and help to their elderly mothers. *Journal of Marriage and the Family, 45*, 193–303. doi:10.2307/351308

Morgan, L. (2012). Paradigms in the gerontology classroom: Connections and challenges to learning. *Gerontology & Geriatrics Education, 33*(3), 324–335. doi:10.1080/02701960.2012.679370

Moss, W. G. (1978). Humanities, aging and the public. *The Gerontologist, 18*(6), 581–583. doi:10.1093/geront/18.6.581

Nussbaum, M. C. (1998). Exactly and responsibly: A defense of ethical criticism. *Philosophy & Literature, 22*(2), 343–365. doi:10.1353/phl.1998.0047

Oró, M. (2009). Female aging: between fiction & real life. *Journal of Aging, Humanities, & the Arts, 3*(3), 222–233. doi:10.1080/19325610903134488

Paige, D. D., Rasinski, T. V., & Magpuri-Lavell, T. (2012). Is fluent, expressive reading important for high school readers? *Journal of Adolescent & Adult Literacy, 56*(1), 67–76. doi:10.1002/JAAL.00103

Port, C., & Swinnen, A. (2014). Age studies comes of age. *Age, Culture, Humanities, 1*(1). Retrieved from http://ageculturehumanities.org/WP/from-the-editors

Posner, R. S. (1997). Against ethical criticism. *Philosophy & Literature, 21*(1), 1–27. doi:10.1353/phl.1997.0010

Pratt, J. R. (2010). *Long-term care: Managing across the continuum* (3rd ed.). Burlington, MA: Jones & Bartlett Publishers.

Rasinski, T. V. (2003). *The fluent reader: Oral reading strategies for building word recognition, fluency, and comprehension*. New York, NY: Scholastic Professional Books.

Rasinski, T. V., & Padak, N. (2000). *Effective reading strategies: Teaching children who find reading difficult* (2nd ed.). Columbus, OH: Merrill/Prentice Hall.

Rosenblatt, L. M. (1983). *Literature as exploration* (4th ed.). New York, NY: Modern Language Association of America.

Rosenblatt, L. M. (1995). *Literature as exploration* (5th ed.). New York, NY: Modern Language Association of America.

Rubin, R. J. (1990). *Of a certain age: A guide to contemporary fiction featuring older adults.* Santa Barbara, CA: ABC-Clio.

Salinger, J. D. (1951). *Catcher in the rye.* Boston, MA: Little, Brown and Company.

Schwarz, G. (2006). Expanding literacies through graphic novels. *English Journal, 95*(6), 58–64. doi:10.2307/30046629

Sheehan, S. (1984). *Kate Quinton's days.* Boston, MA: Houghton Mifflin Company.

Sheets, D. J. (2013). Editor's introduction. Symposium: Popular literature on aging. *The Gerontologist, 53*(6), 1060–1070. doi:10.1093/geront/gnt116

Sullivan, T. A. (1982). Introductory sociology through literature. *Teaching Sociology, 10*, 109–116. doi:10.2307/1317001

Tice, C. J., Harnek Hall, D. M., & Miller, S. E. (2010). Reducing student bias against older adults through the use of literature. *Educational Gerontology, 36*(8), 718–730. doi:10.1080/03601270903324008

Toman, M. (2008). Teaching Dickens's *hard times* in a general education humanities course. In C. C. Irvine's (Ed.), *Teaching the novel across the curriculum: A handbook for educators* (pp. 194–203). Westwood, CT: Greenwood Press.

Waxman, B. (2005). Teaching cross-cultural aging. *Gerontology & Geriatrics Education, 26*(1), 77–95. doi:10.1300/J021v26n01_06

West, R. (1993). *Narrative, authority, and law.* Ann Arbor, MI: University of Michigan Press.

West, R. (2015). Economic man & literary woman: One contrast. In L. Ledwon's (Ed.), *Law & literature: Text & theory* (pp. 127–136). New York, NY: Routledge.

Winston-Salem State University Strategic Planning Commission. (2010). *Achieving academic distinction: The plan for student success.* Winston-Salem, NC: Winston-Salem State University.

Wolf, M. A. (1987). Human development, gerontology and self-development through the writings of May Sarton. *Educational Gerontology: An International Quarterly, 13*(4), 289–295. doi:10.1080/0360127870130401

Zeilig, H. (1997). The use of literature in the study of older people. In A. Jamieson, S. Harper, & C. Victor (Eds.), *Critical approaches to ageing and later life* (pp. 30–48). Milton Keynes, UK: Open University Press.

APPENDIX A

Kate Quinton's Days Analysis

Over the weeks that you are reading *Kate Quinton's Days* you will be analyzing the story. Make notes to yourself as you read so that you will remember key points. I suggest the following:

- Keep a timeline of events. (See example of timeline attached). I suggest using one page for each chapter.
- Keep a log of the characters, their jobs, and relationships to Kate, and your opinion of them based on what is written within the book. (See example attached). I suggest using one page for each chapter.
- Look at the inflation calculator [http://www.dollartimes.com/calculators/inflation.htm] for an analysis of what the differing monetary calculations would be per 2012/2013 dollars.
- Look up as much data as you can for current pay rates, numbers, etc. (You can Google much of this information and locate it that way).

At the end of the semester, we will all discuss what we found. You will need to bring your notes with you to the final class so we can talk about the book.

In addition to your notes you will write a research paper about the book including what you gleaned from the stories, how the book/stories relates to your life/occupation or even to people you know, and what theories/concepts within your textbook apply to Kate's life. As a gerontology student, you should also be able to discuss the family relationship dynamics and various terminologies that we use to describe some of the situations.

Each paper will be individual ... there is no template! You will turn in your notes, your timeline, and your research paper the day after the last class meeting by uploading it to Blackboard. This will allow you to consider how your classmates viewed the book in relation to your views and incorporate their concepts into your final paper. I would expect no less than 8–10 pages typed pages (excluding references and title page) in APA formatting (12 pt font, DS, 1" margins).

Name: _____

Worksheet for timeline/event

Chapter	Date	Page Introduced	Event	Your Impression of Event
1	2/24/1982	1	Beginning of story	Clearly KQ was not well
1	1/5/1982	1	KQ admitted to Lutheran Medical Center (Brooklyn)	

THE 'OTHER' IN OURSELVES

Name: _____

Worksheet for log of the characters (person), the page number where the person is introduced, their relationships to Kate, their job, and your opinion of them based on what is written within the book.

Chapter	Person	Page Introduced	Relationship to KQ	Job	Your Impression of Person
1	Claire	2	Daughter		
	Mario Rossi	2	Landlord		
	Dr. William Ruffolo	2	KQ doctor		Very busy
	Dr. Edward Batzel	3	Dr. on call	Makes house calls	Did his job and that was it. I did not like that he told Claire to call ambulance.

Name: _____
Money transactions:

Chapter	Page	Date	Money Transaction	Recalculate Into 2014 Currency	Your Impression of Event
1		1/5/1982	$40	$99.17	Dr. Batzel's bill
			$90	$223.13	Ambulance ride to hospital

APPENDIX B

Weekly Reflection Prompts—Graduate Class

Your reflective narratives for *KQD* should provide me a benchmark for your understanding of the novel and its content as well as your comprehension and analysis of class content that you are to integrate.

Consider the following as you craft your weekly reflection and discussion:

- What did I learn from this chapter?
- How does this chapter relate to the class content?
- What was surprising or new to me?
- What would I change if I were part of the management team?

Remember to frame your narrative around the human side of long-term care—what the field is now referring to as long-term services and supports and the six criteria from your text, "Long-Term Care: Managing across the Continuum" (Pratt, 2010):

- Criterion I: The long-term care (LTC) system should be based on recognition of the needs, rights, and responsibilities of individuals;
- Criterion II: The LTC system should be easily accessible;
- Criterion III: The LTC system should coordinate professional, consumer, family, and other informal caregiver resources;
- Criterion IV: The LTC system should be an integral part of the health and social system to promote integration, efficiency, and cost-effectiveness;
- Criterion V: The LTC system should be adequately and fairly financed;
- Criterion VI: The LTC system should include an education component to create informed consumers, providers, reimbursers, and regulators.

Teaching Through Remembering: Using Written Reminiscences in Courses for Older Adults

ELENA BENDIEN

This article presents the use of reminiscence work in educational courses for older adults. The author analyzes a course that addresses experiences of time and the process of remembering at a later age. The study demonstrates how reminiscences, written by participants of the course, are used as illustrative material for some of the theoretical points. They are also instrumental in unfolding an answer to one of the key questions of the course, which is, what is the meaning of remembering in later life? The author argues that an educative use of personal reminiscences can improve the insight of the participants in theoretical issues at hand and can help them to develop new social skills, thus enabling them to translate experiences of aging into a sense-making process in later life. In addition, an educational application of reminiscence work broadens the possibilities for the participants to strengthen their feeling of belonging and to reach beyond one dominant version of history.

INTRODUCTION

Education for older people helps them to deal with the fundamental issues of sense making in later life and facilitates the development of new social skills. Such education often relies on self-reflection, which, when not at hand, must either be learned or activated (Housden, 2007; Randall, 1996). Each course that is directed toward a deeper understanding of human life, or—as in our case—of the remembering process and human aging, will benefit from teaching methods with a narrative orientation. As Polkinghorne (1996) asserts, knowing something narratively means making a connection between the issue at hand and a larger picture or episode, especially when the events and experiences of your own life are subject matter of investigation.

Educational courses for older adults can benefit from lifelong experiences of the participants, notably in academic fields that reach beyond evidence-based domains. One can think about the courses on the philosophy of aging, cultural aging, or any other field where the study of aging overrides its biological interpretation and moves into domains of discourse, performance, symbolic representation, memory, and (personal) history. Within those fields the merits of storytelling, autobiographical writing, oral history, and drama have already been investigated for some time (Rossiter, 2002).

This article addresses the use of written reminiscences in a course for well-educated older adults. The goal of the article is to demonstrate the potential value of using personal memories in courses that aim at understanding the experiential and existential aspects of aging. Our objectives are (1) to introduce reminiscence work as an educational tool, (2) to describe and analyze a specific example whereby written reminiscences are used within an educational course for older adults, and (3) to elaborate on the advantages as well as the potential drawbacks of reminiscences in gerontological education. We start with an introduction of teaching with a narrative orientation and proceed with a description of a course, during which the participants were invited to write reminiscences. We explain the nature of the course, the written task, and its purpose. The application of the material that was collected is discussed. After the analysis of the written material and its incorporation into the course, we shall elaborate on the potential of memory work in educational programs for adults.

TEACHING WITH A NARRATIVE ORIENTATION

Several theoretical frameworks, including a narrative orientation toward teaching (Randall, 1996, 2010), transformative learning (Taylor, 2008), and autobiographical learning and reflective activities (Powell, 1985) have inspired this study of the use of personal reminiscences in a course on remembering and aging.

Geriatric and gerontological education often aims at defying or handling the consequences of aging. Randall (2010) calls those approaches "functional modes," which show "how to do things ..., so we can delay our inevitable decline" (p. 25). They usually address topics like diet and nutrition, exercise, and weight control. However, those educational programs rarely treat the nonphysiological processes of aging, such as appreciation of time, spiritual development, new possibilities of learning, and resilience. The course that is discussed here aims to fill this lacuna. It relies on self-reflective learning, with a narrative orientation. McAdams (1996) provides us with the psychological background for the narrative orientation in teaching and learning. He suggests that narration about one's life can be presented in stages. Old age coincides with what he calls the "postmythic" stage, when the plot of life has been more or less revealed and is in need of integration and evaluation. In the interpretation of Randall (2010) it is "a retrospective period in which 'making a living' ... is less pressing an agenda than 'making sense'" (p. 29). This stage of making sense can be also seen as a way to continue writing your own life story. As the data show, evaluation and reevaluation of past experiences does not prevent the process of self-storying, but it can give it a new purpose and direction. Another important premise of narrative orientation is its focus on the experiential aspect of human development, that is, on how people perceive and interpret changes during their lives. Clark and Rossiter (2008) argue that adult education with a narrative approach is based on the inherent connection of the learner with her or his experience, which can be called a "prelinguistic" or tacit experience. When adults use language they attach a meaning to their experiences (p. 64). If "languaging" is done in writing, a productive transformation of the experience takes place. Clark and Rossiter (2008) call writing "a way of making our thinking visible" (p. 67), by means of which the learners can search for coherence in their life stories. A good example is autobiographical learning, that is, learning about ourselves from the experiences we accumulated during our lives. Self-reflection is a key tool to interpret life experiences and to integrate them into our knowledge about the aging process. The transformation that educators may hope to achieve by applying this approach is from experiencing the aging process as an inevitability of "getting" old into consciously "growing" old (Randall, 2010).

One of the teaching strategies that is based on a narrative approach involves memory and reminiscence work (RW), which can be particularly beneficial in courses for older adults (Chandler & Ray, 2002). In contemporary academic and popular discourse, *reminiscence* can mean a social activity, an instrument of self-narration, or a therapy for people with psychiatric or memory problems. RW finds its theoretical background in cognitive and developmental psychology as well as in studies of mental health and depression (Webster & Haight, 2002; Westerhof, Bohlmeijer, & Webster, 2010). The concept of RW has been also explored and applied in studies of autobiographical memory and oral history (e.g., Gibson, 2011). Although the studies that focus on the therapeutic value of RW dominate academic research, the investigations of everyday reminiscences still lag behind (Bendien, 2015). The educational value of reminiscences, that can offer a solution to present-day problems, is generally recognized (see, e.g., Merriam, 1993; Moody, 1988). Less has been said about the specific potential of RW as a teaching technique for care professionals (Puentes, 2000) or older adults (Housden, 2007; Wolf, 1998). This is what this article is set to explore in further detail. Our premise about the teaching potential of reminiscences is based on the reconstructive character of remembering, which in later age is often accompanied by processes of reevaluation of experiences and their re-integration into one's life history (Bendien, 2010, 2012).

DESCRIPTION OF THE COURSE: CONTEXT AND DATA COLLECTION

The course The Art and the Craft of Aging: Time Experience and Remembering Processes in Later Life was developed for the Hoge Onderwijs voor Ouderen (higher education for older people) program at the Radboud University in Nijmegen, the Netherlands. This educational program is countrywide and provides higher education for older people. The courses are given at a university level for anybody who is age 50 years or older. The courses are held twice a year.

The overarching goal of the course we are referring to is to make the participants acquainted with various theories of aging, time experience, and remembering at a later age. The specific teaching goals are activate the ability of self-narration and self-reflection regarding one's personal experiences of aging and remembering, learn how to translate the theoretical framework of the course into everyday experiences of aging and RW, and develop the capacity to accept the changing nature of memories without losing the sense of continuity of one's identity. The underlying educative aim is to regard past experiences as a mobile "life capital" (the term used by one of the course participants), which is valuable for the present and for the future. Aging and time are approached as multidisciplinary concepts, but the course focuses on the sociopsychological and cultural aspects of time experience (vs. chronological time) and remembering in later life. During the lectures the participants jointly search for answers to the question whether loss is a dominant characteristic of aging and whether remembering in later life is just a pastime or forms an intrinsic part of a meaningful life? The main topics that are treated during the classes are the relationship between personal and collective memories, various functions of reminiscing; understanding one's identity through the processes of continuation and change, and discussions about the authenticity of memories and the ethics of remembering. The participants learn to observe how memories surface and how the remembering process unfolds when facilitated by pictures, old-fashioned artefacts, or physical environments that re-create the past. The discussion is built around the dynamic aspects of memories, which leads to one of the main themes of the course, namely, the reevaluative character of reconstructed memories. For the participants to process these ideas, they are invited to engage with their own narratives and experiences. Most of the course themes can be found in the written accounts of the participants.

The course we are referring to consists of six meetings, during which lectures and interactive discussions take turns. So far the course has been given four times. The size of the group in 2011 was 45, in in 2012 was 27, in 2013 was 35, and in 2014 was 15. The age of the students fluctuated between 55 and 83; the average age was 71.4 years. During 2011 to 2014 the gender distribution remained almost the same: 38% of the participants were men and 62% were women. The nonobligatory task to write down reminiscences resulted in a total of 35 texts (from 35 participants). Thirty percent of the participants sent their written reminiscences. Almost all of the texts have been used during the course as illustrations or as material for discussion. The available data consists of the course material, written texts, and field notes about how the participants reacted to (their own) reminiscences that were presented in class. The data was anonymized, and the participants whose written reminiscences are used in this article all gave their written consent to do so, which exempts the use of the data from obtaining further permissions.

The theoretical material of the course, namely, the role, functions, and meanings of the remembering process in later life, is exemplified by personal reminiscences that were presented by the participants. Reminiscences were used as a teaching tool because they provide a rich source for studies on the meaning of remembering. During the course "personal knowing" and "abstract knowing" become integrated, which as we see, provides a fruitful basis to achieve the teaching goal of the course (Randall, 1996).

PROCEDURE

The "task" to write down a random memory was presented as a nonobligatory request, but the participants tagged it as homework. Each time they asked questions about the nature and the topic of the "expected" reminiscences, which reflected a certain degree of confusion. This can be explained by the educational approach that the participants experienced during their youth, when learning tasks were often strictly defined, whereas creative or self-reflective assignments were facultative. This feeling of uncertainty disappeared as the course progressed and mutual trust developed, within the group and between the lecturer and the participants. Most of the written memories were presented by e-mail, the others were handed over during the classes. The texts were used during the last two lectures as illustrations of the key course topics.

The texts were analyzed in three consecutive steps in terms of content and discourse analysis. This approach provided a rich account of the themes, the style, and structure of the written reminiscences. This allowed us to recognize interdependencies between the course material (themes, concepts) and the topics used by the participants.

Content Analysis

First, an open coding was applied to all texts (37 codes), followed by axial coding resulting in four major groups (Table 1). The coding was conducted by one coder. Each text provided multiple codes, and in several cases the same abstract was given several codes. The first and largest group of themes refers to a specific period in the past, mostly childhood (76% of the cases). The second large group deals with the specific value of a memory or

TABLE 1 Open and Axial Codes and Thematic Interdependencies With the Course Material

Axial Codes	Open Codes	Frequency in the Texts, $n = 35$	Thematic Interdependencies With the Course Material
Importance of remembering a specific period of life or a specific theme	Childhood memories	21	Reminiscence bump
	Marriage in later life	1	Aging as continuous development/ageism
	Devotion	4	
	Memories about parents/grandparents	16	Reminiscence bump
	Memories about the death of somebody who was dear	7	Life-defining events
	Fear as a child/betrayal	7	Life-defining events
	School memories	9	Reminiscence bump
	Memories about important life moments	5	Life-defining events
	Memories about war/hunger	3	Life-defining events
	Humor	5	
	Memories about religion and believes	6	
General or specific value of remembering or a specific memory	General value of memories	13	Meaning of remembering
	Reevaluation of an experience	15	Reevaluation
	The value of bad/traumatic memories	7	Clinical applications
	Pride in own achievements	4	Generational memory
	Application of an experience in the present	1	Transfer of knowledge/generativity
	Memories as a token of respect/love for those who passed away	10	Loss and memory
	Shame for some actions of the past	2	Re-evaluation, continuation and change
	Memory as a challenge	6	Totality of memory, identity and memory
	Memory as identity	4	Identity and memory
	Remembering trauma	6	Identity and memory
	Becoming older: pro and contras	1	Aging well
	Reflection on the speed of life changes	1	Chronological versus personal time
	The link between generations	4	Transfer of knowledge/generativity

(Continued)

TABLE 1 Open and Axial Codes and Thematic Interdependencies With the Course Material (*Continued*)

Axial Codes	Open Codes	Frequency in the Texts, $n = 35$	Thematic Interdependencies With the Course Material
Reflection on the process of remembering	Looking in books for answers about meaning of memories	2	Self-reflection, self-development in later age
	We never forget, we add to	1	Totality of memory
	The necessity to share a memory	4	Collective and personal remembering
	False memories/authenticity of memories	1	Ethics of remembering/authenticity
	Process of remembering/reconstruction	12	Reconstructive character of remembering
	Continuation and change of experiences	9	Continuation and change
	Changing self-image	10	Continuation and change
	Self-reflection (in relation to remembering)	15	Self-reflection, self-development in later age
	Art/artistic means and memory	6	Facilitators of remembering
	Cascade of memories/flashes	3	Modes of remembering
	Remembering with help of pictures/objects/spaces	6	The role of objects and spaces
Influence/importance of the course	Application of the course in everyday life	5	Application of the course
	Course evaluation	4	Evaluation of the course

remembering. Among the examples 53% of the content is spent on reevaluation of experiences, on dealing with the loss and acceptance of the consequences of aging. The third group of themes addresses the process of remembering itself. Seventy percent of the examples are about the reconstructive character of remembering and about changes in the self-image and world views. The fourth and smallest group contains themes directly linked to the evaluation or application of the course material itself.

Discourse Analysis

During the second stage the stylistic and structural patterns of the texts were discerned and brought into relation with the codes that were selected. The discourse analysis overrides the boundaries of written material and includes interaction in a social environment of the educational setting as an intrinsic part of the interpretative work (Taylor, 2001). Each text is treated as potentially illustrative material that can promote a mastering of the course content. The variables that have been taken into account are: structure of the text (introduction, one or multiple plots, reflections, conclusions etc.), affinity with a certain genre (story, essay etc.), chronology of the narrative (a single or several parallel or multiple timelines), and the position of the author (as a narrator, a protagonist, or both). The discourse analysis resulted in identification of four modes of narration, namely, the author mode, the mixed (author and commentary) mode, the commentary mode, and the application mode. The modes were titled according to the position that was taken by the author of the narrative. Each mode has specific characteristics in regard to all variables listed above. In the next paragraph each mode is described in more detail. This typology is applicable to the data of this study. It is indicative because the texts often contain elements of several modes of narration at the same time.

Thematic and Stylistic Connections

The purpose of the third step in the analysis was to establish patterns between the narrative modes and the content of the texts, which could reflect the participant's command of the course material. An additional focused coding of the theoretical concepts helped to identify interdependencies between the content of reminiscences and the course material. The major correlations include life-defining events, reevaluation of past experiences, continuation and change in relation to identity, collective remembering, transfer of knowledge, self-reflection, and self-development at a later age and the role of objects and spaces in remembering.

During the courses that were held so far reminiscences were applied as illustrations for various theoretical points of discussion. The results of those applications will be addressed in the following section, organized in accordance with four narrative modes.

APPLICATION IN THE COURSES

Author Mode: Once Upon a Time

The first group consists of 13 texts. 11 participants described their experiences from the first-person perspective. One participant chose to make a written account called "Still Life" about the life of his friend who passed away. Another participant wrote a fairy tale about memories called "Wrinkle story." The author mode was mainly used to tell a story. The similarity of the texts from this group with storytelling as a literary genre is confirmed by the inclination of the participants to title their story, for example, "Händel's Largo," "The blue bucket," "Memory without memories," to name just a few of them. The task appealed to the artistic capacities of the participants who chose to present their reminiscences in the form of a popular literary genre, which had not been part of their assignment. Introductory paragraphs were often used to submerge the reader into the world of the past, but the voice of the present-time author who is evaluating that past is strongly present:

> 1. Traditionally, after the primary school I had to go to boarding school. That period between 1957 and 1961 I did not enjoy very much. My parents, my brother and my sister too received their secondary education at a boarding school. That was a token of the time. (Extract from the text "Memory Without memories")

> 2. You probably know it, the blue enameled bucket. It had the inscription "Vegetables" on it, painted in beautiful gold letters. Inside it was white/grey. It was a practical bucket; the cover for a big pan fitted on top of it precisely. Later I saw it standing on the oil stove where the girls' pads (as a boy I didn't know better) were boiled. When I see this bucket my thoughts go back to the year 1944. (Extract from the text "The blue bucket")

These abstracts show a coexistence of the present self and the self of the narrator that emerges from the past. This feature can be traced to one of the important themes that was discussed during the courses, namely, how our self is embedded in the processes of continuation and change. The participants often begin the course believing that they retain more or less the same identity throughout their lives. When they write down their reminiscences they already prepare themselves to embrace the fact that the process of change must go much deeper, and that it is continuous by nature. These examples were used to show how things that seemed normal and acceptable many years ago are looked at differently today, which is in fact the result of the very important process of reevaluation, one of the core aspects of remembering in later life.

The first extract comes from the reminiscence about misused power and betrayal, as a result of which part of the narrator's childhood memories was lost. The text introduces two different versions of the narrator, that is, a naïve and trusting girl from the past and a strong and independent woman who is prepared to confront one of the most challenging moments in her life. The narrator came up to me during the break, after I had used her story, saying that in spite of her permission she had felt confronted when the story had been read aloud. But in the end the reaction of the group, that showed a sincere sympathy with the feelings of the girl and an uncompromised censure of the cruelty of her educators, balanced the narrator's feeling of unease.

The text about the blue bucket is narrated in a much lighter tone. It transpires humor, though it tells about the "hunger year" during the war. The story has a multilayered temporal structure, which offers a good illustration for a discussion about experiencing time at a later age and the relationship between personal and collective memories. As we have seen, the author commences the tale in the present. Then he leaps into the past, describing the queue of people waiting for food in front of the village butcher's shop. The depiction of the sickening sweet smell of the food is tangible. And finally the last time jump brings the author into 1963 when he suddenly recognizes that same smell and realizes that this is the smell of cattle fodder.

Reading these stories to the participants is an experience in itself. While listening to that reminiscence the participants laughed together, they nodded in recognition, and at the end there was a general sound of exhalation, a mix of surprise, shock, and relief at the same time. Those are important moments, when illustrations that are attached to theoretical concepts help the participants to restore their feeling of authority by valuing the skills, knowledge, and experiences of their own generation. Using personal texts as examples enables us to provide a unique color to the theoretical part of the course as well as to teach the participants self-reflection, freed from an unnecessary bias or shame.

Author and Commentary Mode: Between a Story and a Thought

The second group consists of 14 texts, which represent experiences from the past and the present that are accompanied by self-reflective and evaluative comments of the narrators. The most striking feature of those texts is their almost identical structure. The participants start with a short introduction, in which they address the theme or the task at hand. It is followed by a text consisting of one or several reminiscences. And it ends with a reflective or evaluative comment concerning either the content and the meaning of the memory or the way in which the reminiscences have surfaced.

> 1. Becoming older. You realize it only when somebody else makes you aware of the fact that you have passed a certain mark, after which everything takes more effort, both physically and mentally speaking. The speed decreases ... hypes become less important, you cannot keep up with technical development, with contemporary behavior codes. In short, the future belongs to the young.

> 2. Well, three memories that cannot be broken about the loss of a child whom you wanted to keep so much. It is not so that I would not dare to write about many unpleasant recollections, which are also burned into my memory. But a smile plays on my lips now, because I find it great that the good memories surface first for this exercise.

The comments that are presented above refer directly to some of the themes that are discussed during the lectures: the acceleration of the chronologically understood time versus the slowing down in later life, the existential meaning of good and difficult memories for aging well, and the intrinsic connection of each recollection to the needs and purposes of the present and the future.

One of the most valuable aspects of the texts from this group is the explicit effort of the participants to reflect on the process of remembering. This is in fact a first step toward incorporating the course material into their everyday experiences:

> 3. What should you think of? A memory. Each day that lies behind me adds a memory. Those were my thoughts when I sat in the train from Nijmegen to Amsterdam. I looked at the water of the Waal for a while and thought about the stories and diary fragments of Nescio (Dutch author, EB), and continued reading. And after a quarter of an hour I knew it: a landscape as a memory.

The narrator of this extract describes step by step how her reminiscences surface and obtain shape and color, facilitated by the changing scenery from the train window. That specific case is used as an example of how we "select" what we remember, and how remembering can remind us of a photo that is being developed, when features from the past, first vague and colorless, gradually become sharp and detached. This is an eye-opening moment for participants who often think themselves incapable of such a detailed recollection.

While reading the texts to the audience I often use pictures from that same period, with the aim to visualize what they remember. There is always a margin for error in that visualization, which makes my audience laugh, strengthening their feeling of belonging to the same generation, of being a community, being in charge of their past and their lives today.

The texts from this group show a mixture of genres, where storytelling takes turns with personal comments. Only one text of this group had a title, which in fact places it on the boundary between the first two groups. Often there are several small stories woven into the text, sometimes connected by the same theme, sometimes totally disconnected from each other:

> 4. My memories, especially the earlier ones, are stored as short flashes, often without a beginning or an end. There are usually no details, which I am not very good at anyway…. From the primary school time I remember that I was brought under narcosis with a gasmask, and I dreamed that I was constantly turning around the rail with my head down, what we used to do every day on our way from home to school.
>
> From the secondary school I remember the cellar, where we had to park our bikes, put on a skirt over our trousers. Further I remember all kinds of moments from that period as short flashes, but I cannot make a coherent story out of them…. With pictures I can call back more memories from the

time when my children were small. From the periods without or with few pictures.... I don't remember much.

This cascade style is in itself a useful example for when the process of remembering is explained. The narrator switches repeatedly between her flashes from the past and her present comments, and by doing so she constantly assesses her capacity to remember, which appears to be just as important to her as the memories themselves. The last example she gives is about the role of objects for RW. Examples like this teach the participants that artefacts and physical spaces can facilitate and channel memories into specific directions. This realization prepares them for yet another revelation, namely, that artefacts and familiar surroundings can play an important role for aging well, especially when older people have to leave their homes. During the classes the participants talk about their experience with their parents, who already moved from their homes to care facilities. It helps them to anticipate their own emotions and actions for when they will have to move to a smaller place themselves.

Commentary Mode: I Am (Not) My Memories

The third group contains texts with remarks and comments about the remembering process in general and the course in particular. There are four texts, three of which are built around specific memories, whereas the fourth contains a general comment on the value of memories in the narrator's life. The texts from this group demonstrate the sincere interest of the students in the course material, the increasing involvement in the subjects that are discussed, and their critical and constructive stance toward the content. Furthermore these texts provide us with strikingly opposite reflections on the value of reminiscences, which I want to address in more detail:

1. It took me some time to answer your request and to pen down a memory. There are so many of them that have already been reviewed during the past weeks, in my mind. They are all dear to me, because I am my memories.

2. I am doing well: I worked a lot in my life (through self-reflection, with the help of therapy and friends, and also thanks to the training) in order not to be defined by my memories, and to live a good life. I benefit from all that now.

The first extract sums up the experiences of several participants, which they either expressed in their texts or during the course itself. The issue here is whether the participants accept the fact that they are defined by all their memories, including the difficult and even traumatic ones. This is exactly what the second extract brings to light. It is part of an e-mail message that, as an attachment, contained a detailed description of the feelings that the participant had experienced during one specific lecture. A part of that lecture describes an innovative application of RW in one of the care facilities. Slides were shown containing pictures of the Reminiscence Museum, that is arranged as an old-fashioned home, with furniture and paraphernalia from 1890 to 1970. This is one of the sessions during which the participants are always very amused. They engage in the process of recognition collectively, whereby they experience the power of interaction and collective remembering.

The second extract was written by a participant who had difficulties coping with that form of presentation. She describes her feelings as a growing heaviness and unease, which she offsets against the joy and amusement of the rest of the group. The style of her account is powerful and defenseless at the same time. She narrates in the present time, so she literally invites you to feel what she was feeling at the time. Without further explanation she lets you know that her past contains some dramatic experiences, which she has learned to keep a lid on, but which escaped her guard when the course material unexpectedly introduced her to visual material. The description of her feelings is tangible. The style is almost poetic. But the most remarkable part of her account is the description of how she deals with her feelings afterwards, by escaping to nature and quieting herself down with the lullaby:

> Like a ship in the harbor
> like a mother a child
> like a light in the darkness
> I hold you a while
> we'll rock on the water
> I'll cradle you deep
> and hold you while angels
> sing you to sleep

The course focuses on everyday reminiscences. It does not address clinical applications of RW in much detail and discusses only briefly how traumatic experiences from the past are managed. Randall (1996) suggests that when a course deals with people "in transition" (i.e., experiencing a serious change in life) it contains a therapeutic component. This can be true, but we must be clear in defining the boundary between the work of a lecturer/trainer and a psychiatrist. In cases such as the last one, to show respect and empathy is as close as an educator can come to the process of healing.

The written account of the last participant was not used during the course, but it is valuable for us in several ways. Firstly, it cautions against possible negative consequences for older participants that can be triggered by the use of reminiscences that refer to traumatic experiences. Secondly, the way that this particular participant managed to come to terms with her feelings about the lecture material by laying them down openly (to the lecturer) in her text shows a way the course can help people with difficult pasts, especially within a smaller group. Thirdly, the participant's way of dealing with her distress shows how the teaching techniques that are often used in the field of humanities and arts, such as writing a diary, using poetry or music, can stimulate self-reflection and self-understanding.

Application Mode: What Suits the Day

The final group of texts consists of four written accounts, in which the participants try to apply the insight they obtained from the course to their past and present experiences. In one of the texts the narrator consciously reevaluates the story she has just told. Authenticity is of great importance here. The participants discover that, unless purposefully falsified, there are no wrong memories. There are only ever-changing selves that reconstruct memories in accordance with their changing views and convictions.

The texts from this group are integral, as opposed to the reminiscences from the other groups, because we can find elements of various genres there, like a short story, or a commentary with a direct link to the course material:

> My sister is 72 years old and she is a widow. She married a man ... also a widower. They both wanted to keep their memories about their first partner alive. That is why they decided to keep their wedding rings, and to add the second name to it.... I found it very impressive, and it matches exactly what we have discussed during the course: Nothing goes away, but something is added on! By the way, I also made a speech that day, about some aspects of our memories which we had discussed during the course. It was very suitable for that day.

Texts like the one above are usually presented right at the end of a course, but they can be used during consecutive courses. An issue that this particular account raises refers to an important theme within aging studies, namely, the association of aging with personal loss, a decrease in abilities and in social participation. As each day provides us with new memories, so each day can be seen as a precious addition to the way we make sense of our lives, even at a later age. This is something that the participants of the course usually know or hope for intuitively, but they need to hear it explicitly, especially because in many social settings the popular culture propagates the opposite.

DISCUSSION AND CONCLUSIONS

Our examples represent some key themes and modes of reminiscences that were used during the course to illustrate theoretical concepts and to promote discussion. The analysis demonstrates that written reminiscences have an epistemological value that is consistent with the teaching goals of the course as well as with the expectations of the participants. Most of the participants are eager to be challenged by a creative task. The narrative nature of the assignment appears to appeal to them. Their enthusiasm is rooted partly in the universal character of storytelling as a means to explain our identity, but it is also due to the stage the participants have reached in life, when a significant number of them endeavor to create an integral and coherent understanding of their lives (Kenyon, Bohlmeijer, & Randall, 2010). The decision to participate in the course about remembering already reflects a desire to learn how to handle aging, how to re-story yourself with dignity while preserving the integrity of all your memories.

By writing reminiscences and hearing them back when they are used as illustrative material during the classes, the participants learn to accept changes without losing the coherence of one's memory and life story. By doing that they acquire an answer to the question whether reminiscing in later life is just daydreaming or an essential part of sense making in later life. Some of the participants prefer a "down-to-earth" approach and start with a pragmatic explanation of the meaning of remembering, such as the pleasure of remembering or a transfer of knowledge. The fact that the memories are their own reassures the participants in their search for answers, allowing them to proceed as a group in an atmosphere of trust and confidence. A safe environment adds to the emotional side of the learning process in later life, without which the learning goals can fail.

One of the outcomes of the course with narrative orientation is the possibility to value life experiences integrally, that is, as a protagonist, as a narrator, and as an audience at the same time (Randall, 1996). This is important because it allows putting a personal evaluation into perspective and acquiring affinity with those on whom those experiences are bestowed.

The style and genre of written reminiscences show corresponding patterns in the choice of the mode and the theme that the participants dwell on (de Medeiros, 2007) and the way they relate to the course material. Especially the author and the mixed modes reveal some interdependencies. Telling a story often takes the narrators back to their early years. Another route is storytelling about the life-changing, dramatic experiences (loss of a child, betrayal, war). In each case reminiscing often goes hand in hand with a certain degree of romanticizing. The assignment stimulates the creative capacities of the participants, who often turn their reminiscences into a literary work. Their prior knowledge that their texts can be used as illustrations during the course play an important role. As a result they engage with their past in a more creative way, which in turn stimulates in-depth self-reflection and may result in an increase in self-worth, given the positive and supporting reactions of the fellow-participants.

A creative way of responding to the task to write things down underlines one of the most challenging theoretical issues of the course, namely, the fact that our memories belong to the present. The participants learn that even the most powerful memories of the past cannot imprison them within the fixed framework of former views and convictions, because those memories are recreated within a totally different frame of mind, and they may and will be adapted accordingly. This insight allows them to look differently at the authenticity of their memories and gradually accept the changing nature of their selves.

Most of the texts show strong emotions, irrespective of how far away they go back in time. Although emotionally charged reminiscences can improve the understanding of aging, we need to tread cautiously when applying them during the courses, especially where dramatic events of the past are concerned. The role of the educator here is one of a facilitator of "wisdom environments" and a catalyst (Randall, 1996, 2010) of an interaction that includes all the participants. A useful way to promote an environment of trust is to modestly share with the group some reminiscences of your own. And never forget that your participants are all (lay-)experts in the field of aging.

The analysis highlights the significant role of written reminiscences in educative courses for adults. One of the limitations of this specific study is the lack of cultural diversity among the participants of the course. Most of them were White Dutch middle-class residents. The use of reminiscences has a strong pedagogic potential because it stimulates discussion about the diversity of experiences of the past and opens possibilities for coexistence of different cultural versions of history. That last notion could not be attested to during this particular course, which leaves us with a task for a follow-up investigation.

This article allows for a brief insight in the value of written reminiscences for educational purposes of the course and the process of learning among older adult participants. Although the course is built up around analysis of the remembering process, it is intrinsically connected to various aspects of aging, which becomes explicit in the written accounts of the participants. Those personalized experiences improve their capacity of self-reflection and, by extension, an understanding of the complexity of the aging process they are experiencing on a daily basis. A balanced integration of written reminiscences into theoretical courses can produce promising results for the future incorporation of creative techniques from humanities and arts into educational programs for older adults. But more importantly, it can give a voice to the entire generation, for the benefit of which geriatric and gerontological education exists in the first place. Here is one of those voices, summarizing the course and applying its core notions into his world view:

> Memories are my stocks and shares. The value rises and falls according to supply and demand. Some of the shares I don't want to lose. I acquired them when I was young.... They have kept their sheen for me, even though they are worth nothing nowadays. I must admit, I have added a color to them, from my fantasy. Surely, there is nothing wrong with that?
>
> Some of the shares are more of a burden than a pleasure. At times they keep me from enjoying the profitable ones. But even if I should

chuck those worthless shares into the garbage can, they would stick in that indestructible memory of mine. So what should I do?

A solution to that annoying predicament would be to pay more attention to the valuable shares. And to share them with people around me… So I am going to enjoy what I consider to be the most glorious moments of my life. After all they are and will remain my shares. Even though they don't have an eternal value… They are a part of my life, as a source of inspiration to acquire more shares every day.

To simply experience every day as a new chance to add to the capital of my life.

REFERENCES

Bendien, E. (2010). *From the art of remembering to the craft of ageing: A study of the reminiscence museum at Humanitas, Rotterdam*. Rotterdam, the Netherlands: Stichting Humanitas.

Bendien, E. (2012). Remembering (in) the past perfect: Ethical shifts in times. *Memory Studies*, 7, 328–338. doi:10.1177/1750698012439198

Bendien, E. (2015). Cultural projection of dementia in the reminiscence museum. Dynamics of extrapolation. In A. Swinnen & M. Schweda (Eds.), *Popularizing dementia: Public expressions and representations of forgetfulness* (Vol. VI, pp. 163–184). Bielefeld, Germany: Transcript Verlag.

Chandler, S., & Ray, R. (2002). New meanings for old tales: A discourse-based study of reminiscence and development in late life. In J. D. Webster & B. K. Haight (Eds.), *Critical advances in reminiscence work: From theory to application* (pp. 76–94). New York, NY: Springer Publishing Company.

Clark, M. C., & Rossiter, M. (2008). Narrative learning in adulthood. *New Directions for Adult and Continuing Education, 2008*(119), 61–70. doi:10.1002/ace.306

De Medeiros, K. (2007). Beyond the memoir: Telling life stories using multiple literary forms. *Journal of Aging, Humanities, and the Arts*, 1(3/4), 159–167. doi:10.1080/19325610701638052

Gibson, F. (2011). *Reminiscence and life story work: A practice guide*. London, England: Jessica Kingsley Publishers.

Housden, S. (2007). *Reminiscence and lifelong learning*. Leicester, England: Niace.

Kenyon, G., Bohlmeijer, E., & Randall, W. L. (2010). *Storying later life: Issues, investigations, and interventions in narrative gerontology*. Oxford, England: Oxford University Press.

McAdams, D. P. (1996). Narrating the self in adulthood. In J. E. Birren, G. M. Kenyon, J.-E. Ruth, J. J. F. Schroots, & T. Svensson (Eds.), *Aging and biography: Explorations in adult development* (pp. 131–148). New York, NY: Springer publishing Company.

Merriam, S. B. (1993). The uses of reminiscence in older adulthood. *Educational Gerontology*, 19(5), 441–450. doi:10.1080/0360127930190507

Moody, H. R. (1988). Twenty-five years of the life review: Where did we come from? Where are we going?. In R. Disch (Ed.), *Twenty-five years of the life review:*

Theoretical and practical considerations (pp. 7–21). New York, NY: Haworth Press.

Polkinghorne, D. E. (1996). Narrative knowing and the study of lives. In J. R. Birren, G. M. Kenyon, J. Ruth, J. J. F. Schroots, & T. Svensson (Eds.), *Aging and biography: Explorations in adult development* (pp. 77–99). New York, NY: Springer Publishing Company.

Powell, J. P. (1985). Autobiographical learning. In D. Boud, R. Keogh, & D. Walker (Eds.), *Reflection: Turning experience into learning* (pp. 41–51). London, UK: Routledge Falmer.

Puentes, W. J. (2000). Using social reminiscence to teach therapeutic communication skills. *Geriatric Nursing, 21*(6), 315–318. doi:10.1067/mgn.2000.112147

Randall, W. (2010). Storywork: Autobiographical learning in later life. *New Directions for Adult & Continuing Education, 2010*(126), 25–36. doi:10.1002/(ISSN)1536-0717

Randall, W. L. (1996). Restorying a life: Adult education and transformative learning. In J. R. Birren, G. M. Kenyon, J. Ruth, J. J. F. Schroots, & T. Svensson (Eds.), *Aging and biography: Explorations in adult development* (pp. 224–247). New York, NY: Springer Publishing Company.

Rossiter, M. (2002). Narrative and stories in adult teaching and learning. *ERIC Digest, 241*, 1–8.

Taylor, E. W. (2008). Transformative learning theory. *New Directions for Adult and Continuing Education, 2008*(119), 5–15. doi:10.1002/ace.301

Taylor, S. (2001). Locating and conducting discourse analytic research. In M. Wetherell, S. Taylor, & S. J. Yates (Eds.), *Discourse as data: A guide for analysis* (pp. 5–48). Bath, UK: Sage in association with the Open University.

Webster, J. D., & Haight, B. K. (2002). *Critical advances in reminiscence work: From theory to application*. New York, NY: Springer Publishing Company.

Westerhof, G. J., Bohlmeijer, E., & Webster, J. D. (2010). Reminiscence and mental health: A review of recent progress in theory, research and interventions. *Ageing & Society, 30*(04), 697–721. doi:10.1017/S0144686X09990328

Wolf, M. A. (1998). New approaches to the education of older adults. *New Directions for Adult and Continuing Education, 1998*(77), 15–25. doi:10.1002/ace.7702

Aging and the Arts Online: Lessons Learned From Course Development and Implementation

JACQUELINE EATON

With the recent move toward competency-based gerontology education, incorporating humanities and arts will be necessary for accreditation. This article describes the pedagogical approaches and lessons learned during 5 years of development and implementation of an asynchronous online course in Aging and the Arts. Fifty graduate and undergraduate students participated in the course over five semesters. Discipline diversity increased subsequent to designation as a fine arts general education course. Students expressed appreciation for multimedia resources, an initial fear of creating a wiki, and online redundancy was reduced through increased community engagement that also augmented application in real-world settings. The visual nature of arts and aging lends itself to a compelling and interactive online course experience that can be adapted to synchronous, hybrid, and face-to-face formats. Opportunities for community engaged learning will increase as art programs for older adults become more prevalent.

Research and practice in aging and the arts has increased in the past two decades. Arts-based interventions have been linked to enhanced quality of life, cognitive functioning, and social interaction with older adults (Carr, Wellin, & Reece, 2009; Cohen, 2006; Fraser et al., 2015; Hanna & Perlstein, 2008; Noice, Noice, & Kramer, 2014). The humanities and arts promote a holistic view that moves beyond the deficit model of aging while promoting interdisciplinary collaboration that bridges science and art (Cole, Kastenbaum, & Ray, 2000), which benefits students, older adults, and society in general.

In November 2014, the Association for Gerontology in Higher Education (AGHE) adopted competencies for undergraduate and graduate education. Six competencies were identified as foundational to all fields of gerontology, including competency 1.5 The Humanities and Aging (Association for Gerontology in Higher Education [AGHE], 2014). Programs desiring gerontology accreditation will be required to provide evidence that the humanities and arts are represented.

Designed as an asynchronous class for graduate and undergraduate students, Aging and the Arts is an online course that explores enhancing late life potential through theatre, art, film, dance, and music. The purpose of this article is to describe the process of course development and implementation in an effort to provide an example of one method of incorporating the humanities into gerontology programming in higher education.

METHOD

Background

Founded in 1973, the Gerontology Interdisciplinary Program (GIP) at the University of Utah offered a wide variety of courses to support master's degree and undergraduate and graduate certificate programs. However, the program was missing representation of humanities and arts-based approaches to aging. In 2009, one instructor with degrees in theatre and gerontology proposed the creation of an asynchronous online course focused on arts-based approaches to aging.

Course Design and Development

FUNDING

Funding was sought from the University's Technology Assisted Curriculum Center to support development of these materials. The goal was to create a fully online interactive upper-division course for graduate and undergraduate students with the intent of meeting the Intellectual Exploration (IE) Fine Arts undergraduate requirement. A small amount of funding supported development activities including collecting and evaluating readings and multimedia resources, creating engaging lectures using Adobe Captivate, organizing course materials into learning modules, drafting assignments and grading rubrics, planning formative evaluations for student feedback, and obtaining copyright approval for streaming media.

BACKWARD COURSE DESIGN

As part of funding support, an instructional designer provided input in online design and mapping course objectives to activities and assessments. Initial development incorporated Wiggins and McTighe's (2005) backward design model. This process began by identifying the goals as to what students should do, know, and how they might differ upon completion of the course. After documenting these aims, course objectives were drafted to target a variety of learning processes as outlined by Bloom (1956) and Anderson and Krathwohl (2000). Objectives for this course included:

1. Identify approaches to aging through artistic forms, such as theatre, art, film, dance, and music;
2. Connect theories about aging to older adult contributions in the field of art;
3. Examine personal goals and values through the lens of creative aging;
4. Research, collect, and share resources associated with aging and the arts;
5. Demonstrate the ability to utilize artistic knowledge when working with older adults; and
6. Analyze and critique artistic approaches to aging.

At this point a grid was created to identify (1) how to assess student change for each objective; (2) specific teaching and learning activities to prepare students for each assessment; and (3) resources to support teaching and learning activities (Table 1).

Assessments

Assignments were developed to increase interaction and encourage active learning. In an effort to promote online engagement, project-based assessments were developed using a variety of online tools to diversify student interaction. Assessments occurred through formative and summative tasks incorporated into course assignments. These included wiki presentations, discussions, art viewing, and graduate projects in the community.

Wiki presentations. Students were required to create a presentation over the course of the semester; these were shared on a course wiki (Aging and the Arts [Wiki], n.d.). The objectives of these presentations included (1) research and collect a variety of academic and multimedia resources, (2) analyze artistic approaches to aging issues, (3) identify how artistic knowledge can be used when working with older adults, and (4) assess the future trends in aging and the arts.

Students chose a topic early in the semester, such as poetry, music, culture, or dance. Arts-based topics were required; however, students were encouraged to be creative in identifying areas of interest. Those with similar topics were placed in small groups that helped support presentation development. Groups created objectives for their broad topic and peer reviewed project outlines and final presentations. Projects were required to include background to the topic, scholarly research, examples, explanation of how

TABLE 1 Aging and the Arts: Alignment Grid

Learning Goals/Objectives	Ways of Assessing This Kind of Learning	Actual Teaching and Learning Activities	Helpful Resources
1. Identify approaches to aging through artistic forms, such as theatre, art, film, dance, and music	Not graded—online learning module for each topic	Variety of learning modules containing interactive presentations, videos, webinars, Web sites, and readings. Topics cover theatre, art, film, dance, and music.	National Center for Creative Aging Web site Video clips and Web sites Arts and Aging toolkit—online textbook
	Graded—online discussions to demonstrate understanding of readings	View examples and discuss late life reinvention	Online discussion board
	Graded—online discussion about reinvention (Week 8) Graded—online discussion about benefits of dance (Week 9)	Online discussion about benefits of dance, using article reading	Article/Web site—Liz Lerman
2. Connect theories about aging to older adult contributions in the field of art	Graded—online discussion applying of aging and art theory (Weeks 2–3)	View Captivate presentation on aging and art theories Apply aging and art theories to video clip through online discussion	Example of theory application Online interactive theory presentation in captivate Video clip involving older adults
3. Examine personal goals and values through the lens of creative aging	Not graded—online discussion post: introductions	Online discussion—introduce background and purpose for taking course; What is your personal definition of art Week 6 unit on Aging as Art	Class discussion board
	Graded—Week 8 discussion—representations of aging in film	Week 8 discussion—student observations of aging representation in film	Video clip examples: Elaine Stritch, Betty White
	Graded—Week 11 online discussion about enchanting activities		Video clips: *On Golden Pond* and *Grand Torino*

	Not graded—Personal reflection email regarding responses from the Week 1 discussion	Think about civic engagement and "think tank" regarding new ideas for long term care and apply the idea of enchanting activities in online discussion posts Reminder of original course questions, and request to rethink responses. What has changed over the course of the semester?	Long term care think tank
4. Research, collect, and share resources associated with aging and the arts	Graded—Class wiki project	Choose wiki page on topic of choice and organize/post resources relevant, share resources with others regarding their wiki topic.	Class wiki page—chat room/discussion board for group meetings
5. Demonstrate the ability to utilize artistic knowledge when working with older adults.	Graded—online discussion about intergenerational community building (Week 5)	View intergenerational video and discuss creation process.	Online discussion board
	Graded—online discussion about effective aging and art program—identify best practices (Week 6)	Read effective practices working with aging and arts and watch 2 short video examples to start discussion on best practices.	Readings and video on intergenerational work
	Graded—online discussion regarding implementing arts into existing or new programs (Week 9)	Examples of dance programs, philosophies lead to text reading on program implementation	StageBridge/Roots & Branches video and reading
	Graded—senior art viewing paper	Observe art and aging and describe how artistic knowledge is used to work with older adults.	Arts and Aging Toolkit, Liz Lerman and Kairos Web sites
	Graded—graduate project (graduate level only)	Use ideas, examples from course to create an opportunity to integrate aging and the arts. Learning modules provide examples	Post aging and art observation opportunities throughout semester for students—on blog and/or in course announcements

(Continued)

TABLE 1 Aging and the Arts: Alignment Grid (*Continued*)

Learning Goals/Objectives	Ways of Assessing This Kind of Learning	Actual Teaching and Learning Activities	Helpful Resources
6. Analyze and critique artistic approaches to aging.	Graded—discussion to critique age defying performance (Week 4)	Read example of performance; critique reality vs. defying age	Video clip of Palm Spring Follies, and reading examples from Basting
	Graded—Week 7 discussion—compare and critique two programs working with older adults with dementia	Search two program Web sites and compare process of using art as tool to work with people with dementia	Meet me at MoMa Web site and National Public Radio interview regarding Artists for Alzheimer's
	Graded—online discussion comparing two music programs (Week 10)	Online discussion—discusses evaluating programs (examples in course text) and then students practice with a video of a community choir vs. a podcast of professionally conducted choir—both for older adults	Online text, Young@Heart, and Jeanne Kelly Podcast
	Graded—senior art viewing	Readings about critiquing, and evaluating aging and arts programs (as well as practice on the discussion board) will help students assess the program that they choose to observe	Aging and Arts toolkit, Week 4, Week 7, Week 10 help students practice concepts—readings provided in these weeks
	Graded—class wiki project	Analyze resources and post those most relevant to wiki topic.	Class wiki page, learning modules, web resources

Learning modules with examples, Arts and Aging Tookit, Students incorporate materials (video, audio, photo) into wiki.

the art form has been used to work with older adults, and future trends. A variety of multimedia resources were required to make interesting presentations and students were given the freedom to create as they saw fit.

Initially this assignment had few due dates outside of topic choice and final presentation. This was too much creative freedom for the majority of students, so with each year, incremental steps and due dates were added to help them work through the process of creating the presentation throughout the semester.

Toward the end of the semester students were required to peer review other wiki presentations. This gave them the opportunity to incorporate feedback one final time before receiving a final grade.

Discussions. The discussion board provided the opportunity to communicate, question, and demonstrate mastery of course content. The overall objectives included (1) create lively class discussions that demonstrate comprehension of course readings and materials, (2) learn about approaches to aging through art, (3) connect aging theory to various forms of art, (4) analyze and critique class materials, (5) discuss how you can utilize the arts when working with older adults in a variety of settings, and (6) increase understanding of the integration of gerontology and a variety of artistic disciplines.

Two methods were used to meet these goals. First, the instructor replied frequently to students, asking many questions and promoting discussion. Second, students employed roles to move the discussion along. Roles included discussion initiator who posted first, replying with questions to others throughout the week, and writing short summaries to share the main discussion points with other small groups. Midweek discussion due dates, small groups, and group rotations also increased interaction.

Community engagement. The original course included a blog (Aging and Arts: Art Share Blog [Blog], n.d.) that required students to share art resources and post self-reflections on course readings with the goal of incorporating personal values with creativity and gerontology. It became evident that course assignments were writing heavy. Assignment topics may have varied, writing in an asynchronous format for multiple tasks became monotonous.

The blog was replaced with an activity moving students into their communities. All students were required to complete the senior art viewing assignment. This assignment required students to attend at least one form of art involving older adults, such as senior theatre, dance, art installation, or a film about aging and art. This meant that the viewing was created by older adults and included older adult participants. Students wrote a paper about the experience, making connections with class learning material, and submitting images (i.e., images of them attending, meeting the artist, programs, etc.) of their viewing experience to demonstrate attendance. The goal of this assignment was to (1) view one example of art that is specific to older adults,

(2) analyze and critique the art experience in terms of aging theory and research, (3) reflect upon ones' personal reaction to the art, (4) synthesize thoughts with class materials and discussion, and (5) experience current application of art to aging issues. Originally, many students chose to view films focusing on arts and aging. This became problematic when it was clear that it reduced opportunities to interact with the wider arts-based community. The assignment is now limited to in person, face-to-face forms of art.

There was initial concern that community resources would limit the number of opportunities students had to view live performances. This was not the case; students were provided a list of potential community-based opportunities. Students outside of large cities or in a different state worked with the instructor to identify viewing opportunities. Local newspapers, senior centers, and state art agencies provided a variety of resources to help students locate events (National Assembly of State Arts Agencies, n.d.). Senior art viewings included art exhibits, rehearsals of senior chorales or orchestras, dance performances, senior theatre and art classes at local senior centers.

Graduate projects. Graduate-level students were required to complete a community-based project which they incorporated into their wiki presentations. This project blended individual artistic interests with aging issues. Students experienced arts-based approaches to working with older adults in real-world settings. Sharing these projects with the class provided undergraduate students the opportunity to learn from the graduate students' experience. Projects included the use of art as a form of caregiver respite, shadowing an artist in residence at a cancer center, creating ethical wills, touring a senior theatre, and interviewing older adult artists. As students become more involved in the community, the possibility of using this work as a springboard for master's level projects and theses is increased.

CREATION OF TEACHING AND LEARNING ACTIVITIES

The challenge with asynchronous online learning is promoting active rather than passive learning. Active learning experiences in this course emphasized arts-based interventions, creative expression, community building, program efficacy and evaluation. The creative nature of the course material encouraged all participants to think beyond traditional learning experiences.

Activities were identified to prepare students for course assessments. Units were split into the topics of theatre, dance, music, art, and film. Within each unit, learning modules allowed students to interact with material on a weekly basis. These units included weekly objectives, readings, learning activities, module summary, and reminders. Every effort was made to organize content in a manner that interspersed didactic learning with practice and application. Modules incorporated images, Web sites, videos, and sounds to increase the sensory experience of engaging online.

IDENTIFICATION OF COURSE RESOURCES

An exploration of the history and scholarly writings of artists, researchers, and historians in the area of creative aging (Basting, 1998, Basting, 2009; Cohen, 2000; Cohen et al., 2006; Cole et al., 2000; Perlstein, 1998) led to a list of potential resources to support learning activities. At the time, the *Journal of Aging, Humanities and the Arts*, which was published between 2007 and 2010, provided a resource for topics, references, and experts in this area of study.

The unique element to this subject was the amount of material and resources shared through innovative methods and means. A wealth of resources were available online, as community programs reached out and disseminated their work; artists documented their process in new ways and promoted via the Internet. Video, Web sites, interactive exhibits were easily found online; making this topic ideal for distance learning environments. The textbook for this course was *Creativity Matters: The Arts and Aging Toolkit* (Boyer, 2007). This toolkit provided a foundation for understanding the importance of arts-based programs for older adults and discussed effective practices in designing, implementing, and evaluating such programs. A variety of academic readings, online videos, Web sites, podcasts, and multimedia presentations supplemented the text. Scholarly work in arts and aging has grown exponentially over the past decade, and each year there are new and worthy materials (Carr et al., 2009; Fraser et al., 2015). Resources were chosen based on their quality, exploration of new ideas, critical thought, and the ability to encourage readers to interact with topics in new ways. The course was advertised through flyers shared throughout campus and within its home department. As the course was offered only online, it did include an extra online course fee that ranged between $35 and $60.

Evaluation

Since inception, this course has gone through formative and summative evaluation, incorporating feedback from students and peers. The Center for Teaching and Learning Excellence at the University of Utah provided consultation on the course syllabus and materials. Feedback was implemented before the course was initially taught summer of 2010 as a Special Topics course, which provided the opportunity to test the material. Three graduate students completed the course at this time. Although the low turnout was initially disappointing, the semester became an important exercise in piloting a new course. Students received individual attention, and they took the opportunity to provide immediate feedback regarding assignments and course materials. Between 2010 and 2015, two types of course evaluations were gathered: (1) student evaluations and (2) Instructor evaluation.

Student Evaluations

Course evaluations, student presentations, and self-reflections were reviewed to describe the process of course development. All evaluations were written and included structured (course evaluations), semistructured (course evaluations), and unstructured (self-reflections) questions.

Instructor Evaluation

Initial materials were evaluated by one instructional designer, and a second conducted a midsemester review through course observation. Two faculty members, with expertise in teaching in higher education, peer reviewed the course. These structured assessments occurred during Spring 2012 and again in Spring 2013, were documented and submitted to the university's center for teaching and learning excellence, and used in course revisions. Two graduate students conducted observations and reviews of the course as part of a teaching practicum. These included structured and unstructured evaluations of the course. The instructor retained semester logs of activities, journals including self-reflections about course activities and reactions to course input, and lists of potential changes.

Analysis

Evaluation materials were analyzed by the author using a two-phase process. The first phase involved focused reading to identifying the process of course development and revision between 2010 and 2015. This included highlighting descriptions of this process and outlining course evolution. Pattern coding (Saldaña, 2009) was conducted during the second phase of analysis. This involved coding evaluation materials to identify the outcomes from course design and revision. Repeated ideas identified throughout the data were highlighted. Multiple readings were conducted until repetition was no longer documented. All highlighted material was organized based on pattern codes. Each pattern was then analyzed as an individual concept and a description written about that topic based on the codes identified in the previous readings. The most prominent themes relating to lessons learned during the course of development and revision are included in the results section. The University of Utah Institutional Review Board has designated this project as exempt.

RESULTS

Between 2010 and 2015, a total of 50 students participated in the course at five time points (see Figure 1). Eighteen of these students were graduate-level students. Previously an elective course, enrollment increased in 2013 when the course received designation as a fine arts intellectual exploration general

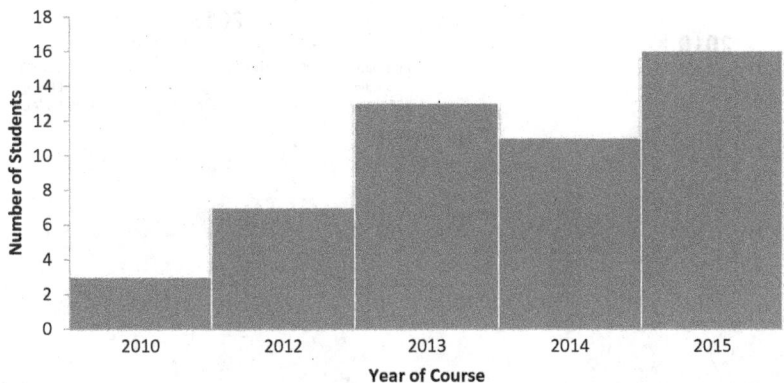

FIGURE 1 Student enrollment in Aging and the Arts.

education course. Disciplinary diversity also increased from two disciplines in 2010 to 11 in 2015 (see Figure 2). Graduate students represented disciplines of gerontology, nursing, medicine, and human development, whereas undergraduate student disciplines included communications, health promotion and education, economics, and international studies (see Figure 3). The course is currently available solely at its home university as well as at the graduate level through NEXus: The Nursing Education Xchange (NEXus, n.d.).

Lessons Learned

Themes from analysis of evaluation materials describe student reactions to the course between 2010 and 2015. These themes characterized the course as challenging but enjoyable, student appreciation for multimedia resources,

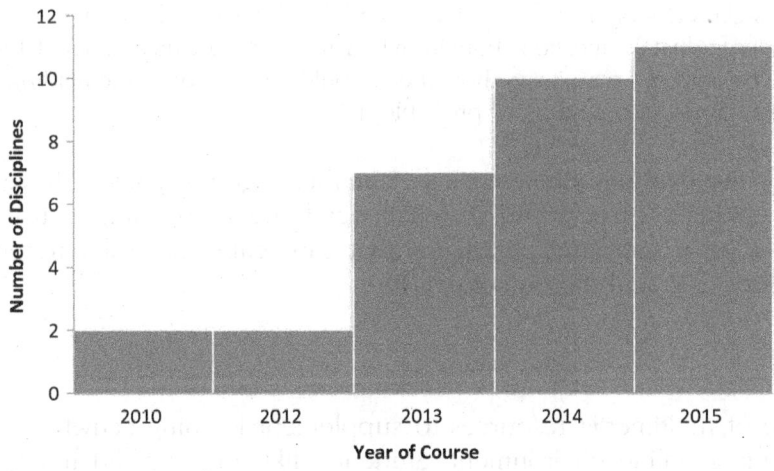

FIGURE 2 Total number of disciplines represented by students enrolled in Aging and the Arts.

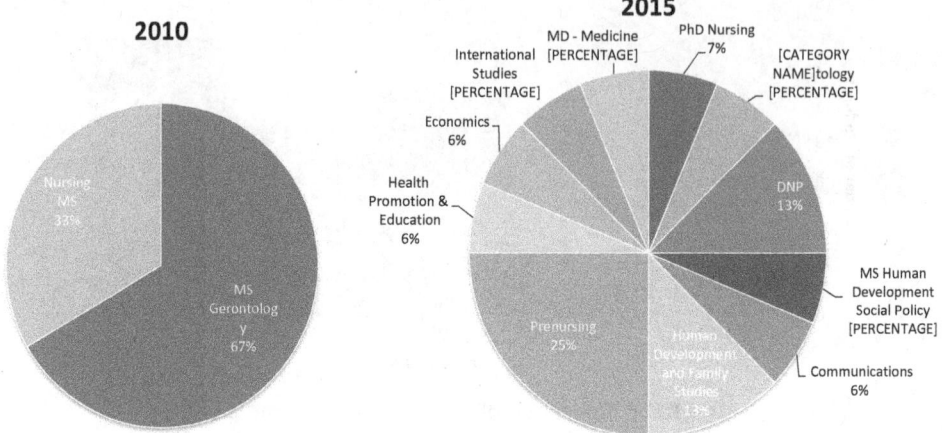

FIGURE 3 Change in disciplinary representation from 2010 to 2015. Disciplines were identified as the program of study students listed at the time of course registration. MS = Master of Science; MD = Medical Doctor; DNP = Doctor of Nursing Practice; PhD = Doctor of Philosophy.

initial apprehension evolved into appreciation for the wiki assignment, and the challenges involved in peer review.

CHALLENGING BUT ENJOYABLE

Students described the course as challenging and overwhelming especially early in the semester when they saw the entire semester of assignments rather than the individual projects broken into small steps assigned weekly:

> This class has been the most influential class I have taken in my entire undergraduate education. Initially when the semester first started I felt overwhelmed. I wasn't sure how there would be time for all the readings, discussions, wiki, and word press blog.

Students described the course as, "the most rigorous course I have taken in my graduate career" and it "challenged me to dig and learn about programs, processes and paradigms that can really make a difference in how people age and their quality of life."

APPRECIATION FOR MULTIMEDIA RESOURCES

The use of multimedia resources to supplement learning activities created an engaging online environment. Students "like that we did not have to buy a book and instead went online to find media resource." The online text was well received:

> I think that the Arts and Aging Toolkit helped me to achieve a deeper, more meaningful ability to critically analyze programs, which gave me a better appreciation for just how effective and successful some of the examples that we have studied are!

Students are challenged to explore recommended media, as well as to search out exceptional arts-based programming for older adults. They identified strengths and weaknesses of what they viewed and gained practice assessing a variety of resources:

> Watching multiple video clips to find just the right one to include on my page was so entertaining, and I probably spent much more time than necessary engrossed in a documentary from HBO about Alzheimer's than I should have! But I am thankful for the excuse to soak up the knowledge.

> I expected this course to be a simple, mindless discussion of how arts could help the elderly. However, this ... forced me to put into reality the things we have learned. By infusing different media, i.e., pictures, videos etc. it created a constant change in teaching modalities. It was like learning in "bite size" pieces.

WIKI: FROM APPREHENSION TO APPRECIATION

Students were initially concerned about the scope and size of the wiki assignment. This feeling changed during the course of the semester:

> I really didn't think I would like the wiki assignment.... It turned out to be one of my favorite assignments.

> It was a good experience to work with others on a project using primarily online communication methods, as this is something that I can envision doing again in the future as a part of a job, or in graduate school.

The Wiki presentations forced students to explore creation and presentation in a new medium. Students described learning "how to embed objects" and "searching for things on YouTube" and "AgeLine." It initiated a sense of creative inquiry and a desire to share:

> One of the ways I think it stands out as being so useful to me is that so much is going online and this gave me ideas of how to creatively share arts and aging ideas with those I work with and volunteer with.

> I found building the Wiki page to be a great experience of using artistic technique in creating an aesthetic that you hope someone wants to view and read and a medium that integrates the content we learned from the

course. I hope this is something you continue to do in future classes because the application really solidifies the concepts, theories and philosophical development of the course.

The majority of students appreciated the opportunity to create, and have "a stake in the course material" which became real when they made it publically available online.

Peer Review

Peer review was one activity built into the wiki assignment. This motivated students to view their classmates' presentations and provide feedback which was then acknowledged and incorporated. Some students found listening and incorporating feedback a challenge:

> Internalizing and acting on some of the peer feedback was difficult. I tried to understand the comments coming from my classmates and to make adjustments bearing in mind the perspectives of those who are viewing my Wiki page without having an emotional response, but some comments felt a little harsh. To provide a critique without suggestions doesn't help me to understand how I could make the necessary edits to meet the expectations of the peer reviewer.

> I probably learned as much peer reviewing as I did working on my own topic, particularly because I was thinking about what I could contribute or how could I help make it better. I enjoyed reviewing some more than others.

Initially, as this was a wiki, peer review included implementing actual changes to others' presentations. However, students were very timid and hesitant to provide this form of peer review:

> I felt uncomfortable making text revisions and change page organization. Since this was a class about arts and creative expression, I thought that each individual worked hard at expressing on their topic in their own creative manner and that I had no rights to go in and change anything.

Taking this into consideration, adjustments were made and peer review posts were added as comments to the wiki page, which allowed all to view the feedback, and faculty to follow up on implementation. Due to these adjustments, students were more willing to participant in peer review:

> I enjoyed having to peer review the other subtopics, I found I looked at each page and learned how other art forms make a tremendous impact on the aging process. Having to critique really required a full

understanding of what the page was presenting, while needing to grapple with the information. It required me to think and really understand, not just look at the page and watch a few videos.

I also appreciated the feedback from other students. Having others available to critique my work helped me to catch errors that I would have otherwise over looked. It also encouraged me to look into the work of my peers, which served as a source of more new and interesting information.

Summary and Recommendations for the Future

At the end of each semester, students were asked to write a self-reflection that included ideas on how to improve the course. Students requested an increased focus on music, inclusion of digital arts, and more cultural diversity throughout the curriculum. One major emphasis was the desire to interact with the wider community:

> I'm so grateful for the Senior Art Viewing assignment. I think often about this group of senior artists at the ... Senior Center I met with and the impact they had on me as they shared their feelings about art.

Many suggested increasing opportunities for community engagement. Student's desire increased emphasis on what was happening in their local surroundings and practical application to real-world settings:

> I believe that future iterations of this project should include more group work and interaction between group members and cross group communication. I believe that the field of gerontology with respect to the venue of healthcare is collaborative in nature. In my mind one of the largest problems facing healthcare today is the lack of coordination between a patient's multiple providers as well as the staff that pertains to each provider. Because of this, I believe that all classes should have assignments that are dependent on their efforts and effectiveness at communicating and disseminating information through a group.

Self-reflections also demonstrated summative feelings about the student experience. These included adjustments in perception of aging, education, and work:

> Oh, I enjoyed watching as others performed or enjoyed looking at the artistic endeavors of others but always pretty much considered myself a spectator of the arts. This class has helped me to see the potential value the Arts have for the aging adult—all aging adults even those who have spent their entire life in the sciences or business or ...

I didn't expect to relate this class so much to my job as being a CNA but I believe that by taking this course it has helped me see things better through the eyes of those I care for.

Yes, I have worked in long term care facilities and knew the caregiver aspect, but I never really thought about the encouragement and creative aspect of the lives of the people I was taking care of. I learned a lot of the different aspects of art and how their application to our aging population can benefit both them and me.

This class has created an awakening that has been a joyful end to my formal education.

DISCUSSION

The visual nature of the arts lends itself to a multisensory approach to online learning that can be adapted to synchronous, hybrid, and face-to-face formats. Aging and the arts is relevant and imperative to improving gerontological curriculum. The course described here specifically targets AGHE competency 1.5 The Humanities and Aging (AGHE, 2014), but activities throughout overlap and provide opportunities to meet competency content in eight other core domains (Category 1 and 2) and two contextual competencies (Category 3) (Table 2). Although this course provides a broad overview of the intersection between aging and the arts, future courses should be created to help students develop, test, and evaluate arts-based programming in a variety of settings. Such curricula would target more of the recommended competencies, specifically 3.5 Arts and Humanities: Promote Engagement of Older People in the Arts and Humanities (AGHE, 2014).

Opportunities for community-engaged learning will increase as art programs for older adults become more prevalent. Each year it becomes easier to identify resources within communities. Networking with leaders and nonprofit programs involved in aging and the arts is vital to increasing opportunities for students to experience enriched community environments that model best practices in arts-based programming (National Assembly of State Arts Agencies, n.d.). The National Center for Creative Aging has a wealth of resources including Communities of Practice (National Center for Creative Aging [NCCA], 2012a), the Creative Caregiving Initiative (NCCA, 2012b), and The Online Artist Training in Arts and Aging (NCCA, 2012c).

TABLE 2 Alignment of Arts and Aging Objectives to AGHE Competencies

AGHE Gerontology Competencies[a]		Aging and the Arts Objectives					
Core Competency	Recommended Competency Content	1. Identify approaches to aging through artistic forms, such as theatre, art, film, dance, and music.	2. Connect theories about aging to older adult contributions in the field of art.	3. Examine personal goals and values through the lens of creative aging.	4. Research, collect, and share resources associated with aging and the arts.	5. Demonstrate the ability to utilize artistic knowledge when working with older adults.	6. Analyze and critique artistic approaches to aging.
1.1	1.1.1		X				
1.3	1.3.1	X	X				
	1.3.4	X	X				X
1.4	1.4.1	X					X
1.5	1.5.1	X	X	X			
	1.5.2				X	X	
	1.5.3	X	X				
	1.5.4		X				
1.6	1.6.2				X		X
	1.6.5				X		
	1.6.7						X
2.1	2.1.1	X	X	X			
	2.1.3					X	
2.2	2.2.1		X			X	
	2.2.2	X					
	2.2.3	X					
2.3	2.3.4	X					
	2.3.6						
	2.3.8	X			X	X	X
	2.3.9				X	X	
	2.3.10				X		
3.2	3.2.2					X	
	3.2.4					X	X
3.4	3.4.1	X		X	X	X	X

Note. AGHE = Association of Gerontology in Higher Education.
[a] Association of Gerontology in Higher Education (2014).

CONCLUSION

During the 5 years of course development and implementation, Aging and the Arts has promoted engagement within the community, use of technology, and application of arts-based approaches to a variety of disciplines. The growth in arts-based aging research and practice provides a catalyst for increased interdisciplinary engagement and enhanced student interest in gerontology. Opportunities for community engaged learning will increase as art programs for older adults become more prevalent and faculty collaborate with local art councils and creative aging communities of practice. This, in turn, will increase the number of students who are capable of incorporating the arts into their own areas of practice, augmenting research opportunities, interdisciplinary collaboration, and the numbers of older adults benefiting from the arts.

ACKNOWLEDGMENTS

Thank you to the University of Utah Gerontology Interdisciplinary Program, Hartford Center of Geriatric Nursing Excellence, and Teaching and Learning Technologies for supporting the creation of this course. Thank you to Scott Wright for providing encouragement, letters of recommendation, and feedback on course development and creation.

FUNDING

This work was supported through funding from the Technology Assisted Curriculum Center (now Teaching and Learning Technologies) at the University of Utah.

REFERENCES

Aging and Arts: Art Share [Blog]. (n.d.). *Aging & arts: Art share.* Retrieved from https://agingandarts.wordpress.com/

Aging and the Arts [Wiki]. (n.d.). *Welcome to Aging and the Arts.* Retrieved from http://agingandarts.pbworks.com

Anderson, L. W., & Krathwohl, D. R. (2000). *A taxonomy for learning, teaching, and assessment: A revision of Bloom's taxonomy of educational objectives.* White Plains, NY: Longman.

Association of Gerontology in Higher Education. (2014). *Gerontology competencies for undergraduate and graduate education.* Retrieved from http://www.aghe.org/images/aghe/competencies/gerontology_competencies.pdf

Basting, A. (1998). *The stages of age: Performing age in contemporary American culture.* Ann Arbor, MI: University of Michigan Press.

Basting, A. D. (2009). *Forget memory: Creating better lives for people with dementia*. Baltimore, MD: Johns Hopkins University Press.

Bloom, B. (1956). *Taxonomy of educational objectives: The classification of educational goals. Vol, 1: Cognitive domain*. New York, NY: McKay.

Boyer, J. M. (2007). *Creativity matters: The arts and aging toolkit*. Retrieved from http://artsandaging.org

Carr, D., Wellin, C., & Reece, H. (2009). A review of arts and aging research: Revealing an elusive but promising direction for the era of the third age. *Journal of Aging, Humanities & the Arts, 3*, 199–221. doi:10.1080/19325610903134496

Cohen, G. (2000). *The creative age: Awakening human potential in the second half of life*. New York, NY: Avon Books, Inc.

Cohen, G. (2006). Research on creativity and aging: The positive impact of the arts on health and illness. *Generations, 30*(1), 7–15.

Cohen, G. D., Perlstein, S., Chapline, J., Kelly, J., Firth, K. M., & Simmens, S. (2006). The impact of professionally conducted cultural programs on the physical health, mental health, and social functioning of older adults. *The Gerontologist, 46*(6), 726–734. doi:10.1093/geront/46.6.726

Cole, T. R., Kastenbaum, R., & Ray, R. E. (Eds.). (2000). *Handbook of the humanities and aging* (2nd ed.). New York, NY: Springer.

Fraser, K. D., O'Rourke, H. M., Wiens, H., Lai, J., Howell, C., & Brett-MacLean, P. (2015). A scoping review of research on the arts, aging, and quality of life. *The Gerontologist, 55*(4), 719–729. doi:10.1093/geront/gnv027

Hanna, G., & Perlstein, S. (2008). *Creativity matters: Arts and aging in America*. Retrieved from http://www.giarts.org/sites/default/files/Monograph_Creativity-Matters-Arts-and-Aging-in-America.pdf

National Assembly of State Arts Agencies. (n.d.). *National Assembly of State Arts Agencies*. Retrieved from http://www.nasaa-arts.org/

National Center for Creative Aging. (2012a). *Communities of practice*. Retrieved from http://www.creativeaging.org/programs-people/communities-practice

National Center for Creative Aging. (2012b). *The NCCA creative caregiving initiative*. Retrieved from http://www.creativeaging.org/programs-people/ncca-creative-caregiving-initiative

National Center for Creative Aging. (2012c). *NCCA online artist training in arts and aging*. Retrieved from http://www.creativeaging.org/programs-people/ncca-online-artist-training-arts-and-aging

NEXus. (n.d.). *NEXus: The Nursing Education Xchange*. Retrieved from http://www.winnexus.org/

Noice, T., Noice, H., & Kramer, A. F. (2014). Participatory arts for older adults: A review of benefits and challenges. *The Gerontologist, 54*(5), 741–753. doi:10.1093/geront/gnt138

Perlstein, S. (1998). Culture builds community: Elders share the arts. *Generations, 22*(4), 72–73.

Saldaña, J. (2009). *The coding manual for qualitative researchers*. Thousand Oaks, CA: Sage.

Wiggins, G., & McTighe, J. (2005). *Understanding by design*. Alexandria, VA: Association for Supervision and Curriculum Development.

Transformative Theatre: A Promising Educational Tool for Improving Health Encounters With LGBT Older Adults

ANNE K. HUGHES

CLARE LUZ

DENNIS HALL

PENNY GARDNER

CHRIS WALKER HENNESSEY

LYNN LAMMERS

Lesbian, gay, bisexual, or transgender (LGBT) older adults are often unaware or fearful of aging services that contribute to greater vulnerability, isolation, and risk when services are needed. In addition, they may perceive or experience bias in health care encounters. Providers may not recognize their own biases or their impact on such encounters. In response, a group of LGBT community activists, aging professionals, researchers, and a theatre ensemble developed an interactive theatre experience, described herein, that portrays challenges faced by LGBT older adults needing services. Goals included raising awareness among LGBT older adults and providers about issues such as the limited legal rights of partners, limited family support, and fear of being mistreated as a result of homophobia. Evaluations and feedback reflected the potential of interactive theatre to engage people in sensitive discussions that can lead to increased awareness, reduced bias, practice change, and ultimately improved care for LGBT older adults.

INTRODUCTION

There is a sizable and growing number of persons in the United States who identify as lesbian, gay, bisexual, or transgender (LGBT). The 2013 National Health Interview Survey found that 1.6% of the population age 18 and older identify as gay or lesbian and .7% as bisexual (Ward, Dahlhamer, Galinsky, & Joestl, 2014). There is substantial diversity within this population specific to gender, race, ethnicity, and other identifiers, but major concerns exist that cut across all sociodemographic characteristics including a history of discrimination and abuse (Garnets & Kimmel, 2003). Although there is currently an unprecedented focus on the rights of persons who are LGBT, oppression and marginalization continue to be significant forces (Byne, 2014). Historically, the public has in large part chosen to either demonize or simply not acknowledge persons who are LGBT (Garnets & Kimmel, 2003). This continues to be starkly evident in many venues, notably in health care. The Healthy People 2020 report (U.S. Department of Health and Human Services, 2015) and the 2011 Institute of Medicine report, *Health of Lesbian, Gay, Bisexual, and Transgender People*, (IOM, 2011) identified the LGBT population as one of the most under-represented and vulnerable groups in terms of health disparities in health outcomes and health care delivery. It is at increased risk for a number of health threats compared to the heterosexual population due in part to health behaviors as well as social and structural inequities (Centers for Disease Control and Prevention, 2015).

These disparities are compounded by the increased prevalence of chronic conditions and need for services associated with aging. Older adults who are LGBT share health-related experiences with older adults who are heterosexual, but they also face unique challenges that are currently not adequately addressed such as fewer family supports, higher rates of depression and substance abuse, high disability rates, and fear of coming out to health care providers (Fredriksen-Goldsen et al., 2013; Kimmel, Hinrichs, & Fisher, 2015). In addition, they often experience or perceive negative bias, based on sexual orientation, in health care encounters. These biases may be explicit, subtle, or unintentional and have serious consequences for health outcomes and quality of life. They range from lack of understanding of nonconforming gender presentations, assumptions of heterosexuality, and disregard for the personal relationships of older adults who are LGBT. Further, most health care service programs assume that all older adults are heterosexual and include few, if any, special policies or practices related to sexual identity, and have staff who are ill prepared to provide care in a culturally sensitive way (Hughes, Harold, & Boyer, 2011; Kimmel, 2013; Stein, Sherman, & Beckerman, 2010).

The last several decades have witnessed slow but dramatic changes such that LGBT rights, distinct challenges, and needs are beginning to be recognized (Kimmel et al., 2015). Among these shifts, evidence is emerging of the benefits of staff training programs to increasing awareness, if not yet system changes (Leyva, Breshears, & Ringstad, 2014; Moone, Cagle, Croghan, & Smith, 2014; Rogers, Rebbe, Gardella, Worlein, & Chamberlin, 2013). This article describes an innovative educational strategy for increasing awareness and cultural sensitivity among health care providers as well as the aging LGBT community so that both can enter into professional relationships in an informed way that maximizes the potential for the best possible outcomes. It utilizes transformative theatre as a springboard, a starting point, to invite dialogue and engage in mutual learning about how to improve health services for older adults who are LGBT.

Transformative theatre is rooted in the work of Augusto Boal who substantially developed the theory and practice of using public theatre to create social change. Author of *Theatre of the Oppressed*, Boal transformed spectators into active participants in the theatre and believed that by doing so consciousness could be raised and they could carry their new awareness into the roles they played in their daily lives (Boal, 1985; Christensen, 2013; Schaedler, 2010). Why use interactive theatre to address issues of bias and discrimination? Whether bias is overt, covert, or even unconscious, theatrical frameworks offer the opportunity to observe human behavior; peel back the layers of defensiveness, rationalization, fear, and guardedness within each of the characters; and to ultimately see their humanity. The theatre experience can engender empathy and create a space in which to imagine new behavior, practice, and policy. In his 1995 book, *The Rainbow of Desire*, Augusto Boal makes the case for theatre as a powerful tool for self-reflection and transformation:

> Theatre—or theatricality—is the capacity, this human property which allows man to observe himself in action, in activity. The self-knowledge thus acquired allows him to be the subject (the one who observes) of another subject (the one who acts). It allows him to imagine variations of his action, to study alternatives. (Boal, 1995, p. 13)

Burgoyne helped establish interactive theatre as effective pedagogy for faculty development in diversity (Burgoyne, Placer, Taulbee, & Welch, 2008). Its use for teaching in therapeutic and educational settings is growing, as it provides a valuable springboard for discussing difficult issues such as sexual and partner violence (Christiansen, 2013; Dill-Shackleford, Green, Scharrer, Wetterer, & Shackleford, 2015; Yoshihama &Tolman, 2015). Skye, Wagenschutz, Steiger, and Kumagai (2014) have used it to develop medical students' skills in breaking bad news to people and evidence exists of its value to interprofessional team building (Salam, Collins, & Baker, 2012), teaching conflict resolution (Meng & Sullivan, 2011), promoting healthy relationships (Fredland, 2010) and empowering youth who are LGBT (Wernick, Kulick, & Woodford, 2014). However, there is very little evidence of its use among older adults who are LGBT.

In response to community concerns about how older adults who are LGBT will approach their care needs and how they will be treated when they try to access care, our project aimed to achieve the following: (1) to develop and implement a community informed educational experience for professionals in aging as well as the LGBT community, (2) to provide an innovative theatre experience for health care providers and students in the health professions that enables them to recognize biased behavior and be empowered to take action to correct it, and (3) to improve the provision of health care and aging services to older adults who are LGBT. This article provides a description of the project, a summary of evaluation findings, and lessons learned.

PROJECT DEVELOPMENT

This project was initiated by two community activists, one male, one female, both LGBT and older than age 60, who were concerned about the invisibility of older adults who are LGBT. "There are no old LGBT people, and no LGBT people who are old!" exclaimed one of them. It was this statement that started the two talking about educating the LGBT community about common challenges faced by older adults, such as chronic health conditions, that can result in people who are LGBT moving into residential care settings. The two sought a method that would get people thinking about all of the real-life necessities needed to navigate the aging process, including the difficult decisions of how and where to live their final years. They felt that a good medium for conveying this information to the local LGBT community would be some type of play or short skits. The two activists were referred to the Artistic Coordinator of the Transforming Theatre Ensemble (TTE) at Michigan State University (MSU). TTE, housed in the Office for Inclusion and Intercultural Initiatives, was founded in 2006 as a tool for understanding how bias plays out in real life.

With interest in the proposal from the coordinator, they were asked to pull together a few people with relevant expertise and experience for a meeting to further discuss the proposal and create a working concept. The activists purposively identified and invited individuals who represented a cross-section of academic and community leaders in the fields of LGBT research, services, and advocacy. In 2012, the group began attending working sessions with the TTE coordinator. All of these individuals shared their common concerns and/or experiences related to accessing health care and aging services, sexuality and gender bias, lack of knowledgeable health care providers, and fear of being forced to live with others in a homophobic facility with no physical or mental protections for the resident who is LGBT. The group spent the next several months talking about how these concerns should be presented to the public while continuing to glean stories and discuss common issues with each other.

The TTE coordinator developed a rough draft of a scripted piece for the group who actively participated in providing suggested edits, after which actors were brought in to read through the revised script. This reading generated powerful reactions from the group, and all agreed that the script was worth developing into a full transformative theatre experience, based on the structure of theatre developed by Augusto Boal. The project received approval from the MSU Office of Intercultural Initiatives to develop the program as an educational tool for various audiences involved in providing care to older adults, as well as to the local LGBT community. MSU has a community outreach initiative within its mission statement, and it was felt that this type of activity would fit into the University's mission. The theatre ensemble hired a cast of actors and began the process of preparing the theatre experience, titled *Aggie's Story*.

Throughout the rehearsal process, the cast reflected on the realities faced by all older people, and people who are LGBT in particular. The actor who plays Aggie identifies as a lesbian and was able to make the issues at the heart of our story real and urgent for the other actors in the room. They came into the room with empathy, but after hearing this actor's real fears for herself and her partner, the cast's empathy had a specificity that brought the goals of the sketch and subsequent dialogue into sharp focus.

No piece of theatre is finished until a preview performance has taken place, that is, it has been tested in front of a select audience of individuals with perspectives that will make the piece richer and more authentic including, in this case, people who identify as LGBT and health professionals. The preview audience is there to tell the cast and director what is missing or what is not quite right. The theatre ensemble gave a preview performance of *Aggie's Story* for a group of approximately 20 scholars, activists, service providers, and community members. The ensuing feedback discussion was rich and full of debate about the necessity of a culture shift in the area of LGBT rights. For example, one scene in the play depicts a physician rubbing on hand sanitizer after shaking hands with the client. It was included to illustrate a biased act, demonstrating disgust with contact with someone who is LGBT. Providers in the preview performance audience were previously unaware of how such an act could be interpreted as bias and were offended by the interpretation because use of hand sanitizer is routine practice with all clients. The diverse perspectives highlighted the need for increased understanding of health care as experienced from the provider and client perspective. There was group consensus on the need to change hearts and minds in such a way as to not alienate audience members but rather raise mutual understanding so that policies, practices, and procedures at all levels shift toward inclusion. Concrete suggestions were made such as having the physician in the sanitizer scene explain that washing hands is routine practice for all clients and also asking a question related to this scene during the interactive time. The preview performance feedback and discussion points were then incorporated into script revisions that further improved *Aggie's Story*.

AGGIE'S STORY

Aggie's Story chronicles the experiences of a lesbian couple in the health care system, after one of them discovers a lump in her breast. The audience sees the agonizing and exhausting reality that Aggie, age 71, and her partner Cheryl, age 59, must face as they interact with several levels of the health care system. With few legal rights, they navigate their way through a maze of microaggressions in a system seemingly designed to marginalize them. The following script excerpt illustrates one such instance:

Narrator: The oncologist diagnosed Aggie with breast cancer and sent her to see a surgeon. During that visit, the surgeon seemed distracted by Aggie and Cheryl holding hands. He wouldn't make eye contact with them. He was dismissive of Aggie's questions. And he rushed through the consultation.

Scene 3

Aggie: I'm not going to that surgeon. We'll have to find another one. How can he cut into my body if he can't even look me in the eye?
Cheryl: But that surgeon is local.
Aggie: He was rude. We'll find someone else. What about the one you found online?
Cheryl: He'll only do surgery at a hospital that's 2 hours from home.
Aggie: So?
Cheryl: I couldn't be there. I'll only be able to take the day of the surgery off of work. You'd be alone for most of the recovery.
Aggie: I can handle it.
Cheryl: Are you sure?
Aggie: Positive.
Cheryl: OK then. You win.
Aggie: For once!

Cheryl squeezes Aggie for a moment, sighs, and they exit.

Aggie and Cheryl are also trying to help their friend, Gordon (age 78), who fears coming out of the closet in the assisted living facility he finds himself in after a bad fall. In ways subtle and overt, it's clear to Gordon that Deer Creek Manor is not a place that welcomes gay people. The stress of hiding who he is leads Gordon to increase his intake of sugary baked goods and to begin smoking cigarettes again after quitting decades ago. After Gordon has a stroke his ability to communicate is greatly diminished. Although he had hoped to move out of Deer Creek Manor with Cheryl and Aggie's help, Gordon's niece steps in to nix their plans. She is Gordon's only next of kin, leaving Cheryl and Aggie helpless to carry out Gordon's wishes:

Scene 8

Aggie sits next to Gordon, holding his hand. Cheryl is on the phone.

Cheryl: I don't care if Elizabeth is listed as his next of kin. They haven't spoken in 14 years! We're his family. *(beat)* No, we're not blood relatives. We're his family of choice. *(beat)* But his doctor gave him clearance to move to Cedar Glen. Can't the doctor just confirm that that's what Gordon wanted? *(beat)* Fine, ok. Fine.

Cheryl hangs up.

Aggie: So that's that, huh?

Cheryl: I don't know what else to do. It's too late to file for power of attorney for Gordon.

Aggie: This is just wrong. Gordon knows what he wants; he just can't get the words out.

Cheryl: We should make sure *we* have documentation. For us.

Aggie: Even if we have the right paperwork, they don't have to honor it. Someone can just decide … just decide to not let you in the room. It doesn't matter what we want.

Aggie leans forward, her head in her hands. Cheryl goes to her.

Cheryl: Keep breathing my love, I'm right here.

THE TRANSFORMING THEATRE EXPERIENCE

The scripted and rehearsed sketch described above is approximately 15 minutes long, though a full transforming theatre session takes anywhere from 90 minutes to 2 hours. It begins with TTE the facilitator giving credibility and context to the piece by describing how the sketch was developed. Then the facilitator lays out the agenda for the performance. The scripted sketch is performed, followed by a dialogue in which the actors stay in character and the audience asks questions and makes observations. This interactive dialogue presents the audience with an opportunity they don't usually have—to get inside the characters' heads; to know their inner thoughts, feelings, and motivations. This theatrical function is called a "time out," in which an audience can ask to speak to one character alone. The other actors put their heads down, and the facilitator explains that the others can't hear, and that the character who is "timed in" is free to share openly.

When the interactive dialogue has worked its way through unearthing the biases and assumptions in *Aggie's Story* from different perspectives, such as in the hand sanitizer scene, there comes a point at which the audience is ready to work toward solutions. The facilitator's job is to keep them in the discussion long enough to get its full benefit, but not so long that the audience is getting bogged down in details. When the majority of the audience demonstrates that they understand the issues and begin to problem solve (e.g., a majority of the audience acknowledges interpersonal and systemic bias embedded in health care systems and policies) the facilitator transitions to small group work, in which the audience works through assigned questions to help them spell out best practices, policies, and procedures that will address concerns raised in the dialogue. They are asked to think on the personal, departmental, organizational/institutional, governmental, and societal levels. The small groups then report out to the larger group and together generate a list of take-away points that the audience members can implement in their lives or their practices.

The wrap-up involves the actors coming out of character and introducing themselves, and then the facilitator identifies specific resources for continued self-education. In particular, they are directed to Harvard's Project Implicit and the Implicit Association Test (Project Implicit, 2011) for help in examining personal implicit or unconscious biases. They are also directed to the myriad of resources available online at Services and Advocacy for Gay, Lesbian, Bisexual and Transgender Elders (SAGE at http://sageusa.org) and The National LGBT Health Education Center (National LGBT Health Education Center, n.d.). The final step is to have the audience fill out evaluation forms. In his book, *Games for Actors and Non-Actors*, Boal (2002) offers a way of thinking about the "end" of an interactive performance:

> When does a session of The Theatre of the Oppressed end? Never—since the objective is not to close a cycle, to generate a catharsis, or to end a development. On the contrary, its objective is to encourage autonomous activity, to set a process in motion, to stimulate transformative creativity, to change spectators into protagonists. And it is precisely for these reasons that the Theatre of the Oppressed should be the initiator of changes the culmination of which is not the aesthetic phenomenon but real life. (p. 275)

DISSEMINATION

Overall, *Aggie's Story* has been presented to more than 300 individuals, primarily future or practicing health care providers at the following venues: the Midwest Bisexual Lesbian Gay Transgender Ally College Conference, Best Practices of Northern Michigan Conference (BPNM), the Michigan Mental Health and Aging Conference (MH &A), the Community Based Ombudsman Nursing Home Transition—HOME Conference (NHT), for three MSU School of Social Work classes, the MSU College of Osteopathic Medicine, the Health Care Association of Michigan, and the Michigan Center for Assisted Living Convention. An effort is now underway to have *Aggie's Story* presented to older adults who are LGBT in the Lansing, Michigan, area.

EVALUATION

Although *Aggie's Story* was not developed for purposes of a rigorous scientific study, it did include standardized evaluations with systematic data collection prior to and immediately following each session. Data were collected from a convenience sample of conference attendees who constitute one of the primary target groups for such an educational experience. As such, analyses of these data provide insights that are valuable to anyone interested in policy and program development that benefits older adults who are LGBT. Pre- and postassessments were administered to all attendees at three of the aging services conferences (BPNM, MH & A, NHT) ($N = 225$) to determine baseline understanding of and practices related to persons who are LGBT and the perceived impact of the play on knowledge, attitudes, and intent to change practice. Responses were collected from 204 participants for a response rate of 91%. Data were not collected on the nonresponders, and no demographic data were collected from any of the participants. Examples of preassessment questions include (1) I currently provide services/work with patients/residents that identify as LGBT... (choose one) *never, rarely, sometimes, often, don't know*, and (2) I understand the particular needs of older people who identify as LGBT... (choose one) *strongly disagree, disagree, agree, strongly agree, undecided*. Examples of postassessment questions include (1) As a result of today's performance, my understanding of the particular needs of older people who identify as LGBT has... (choose one) *stayed the same, increased, greatly increased, don't know*; (2) As a result of today's performance I feel better prepared to provide services to older LGBT clients... (choose one) *strongly disagree, disagree, agree, strongly agree, undecided*; and (3) I plan to use what I have learned today in my work setting... (choose one) *strongly disagree, disagree, agree, strongly agree, undecided*. In addition to these items, respondents had the option to offer open-ended feedback about the theatre experience. Qualitative data from open ended responses and coordinators' notes were evaluated for themes by three coders. Coding was iterative, that is, it was first guided by the survey questions and then by additional concepts which emerged from the data. Concepts were then organized into discrete categories with shared attributes from which common patterns and points of divergence could be identified. Each concept and category was further discussed by the team to debate interpretation of meaning and to reach consensus. Several prominent categories or recurring themes emerged based on the frequency with which audience members raised specific issues and perspectives. The findings and lessons learned are discussed below.

FINDINGS AND LESSONS LEARNED

Prior to each performance, audience members (total $N = 204$) completed a brief assessment of their current practices and self-assessment of their knowledge about older adults who are LGBT. Combined, the audiences comprised providers in the aging services network, providers in long term care, and public mental health providers and administrators. Providers were asked if they currently provide services to older adults who identify as LGBT. Across the three conferences 106 respondents (52%) stated that they never or rarely provide services to older adults who are LGBT, whereas 61 individuals (30%) stated that they sometimes or often did. Thirty-seven respondents (18%) stated they did not know if they served older individuals who are LGBT. One third of the respondents disagreed or strongly disagreed with the statement, "I understand the particular needs of older people who identify as LGBT," while another one third agreed or strongly agreed and another one third were undecided.

After the performance, audience members were asked to provide feedback about its perceived effectiveness to discern changes in knowledge or awareness related to individuals who are LGBT and concerns. Seventy-five percent of respondents stated that their understanding of the particular needs of older people who identify as LGBT had increased or greatly increased. After the performance, 86% ($n = 176$) stated that they felt better prepared to provide services to older adults who are LGBT. In addition, 86% ($n = 176$) agreed with the statement, "I plan to use what I learned today in my work setting."

Guided discussions immediately following the performance, led by the theatre ensemble coordinator, centered on ways in which audience members could take what they learned in the session and put it into action in their workplaces. Audience members identified challenges to improving care in their work settings, such as prejudice on the part of staff, other residents, and residents' families; the lack of education and training of staff; and systems that are hard to change, such as protocols or forms that are not welcoming or inclusive. An example is an intake form that does not offer a full range of relationship status options. The guided discussion encouraged participants to identify specific individual and organizational changes that they can make when they return to their organizations. Participants discussed the need for education of staff, residents, and family members in the areas of cultural diversity and self-awareness. Many also discussed a plan to advocate for older adults who are LGBT in their settings. Systematic changes included changes to the environment to be more inclusive and welcoming, as well as a review of policies, procedures, and language on forms. Respondents also discussed how they can interact more positively with elders who are LGBT by listening carefully, showing respect, avoiding assumptions, reserving judgment, and protecting dignity. Many respondents stated that they would incorporate the new knowledge they gained to improve their practice with older adults.

In the open-ended feedback most respondents were enthusiastic about the play and the guided discussion that followed. Many indicated that they gained valuable information and insight about how bias is experienced by older adults who are LGBT in their everyday interactions with care providers. Some noted that the skit illuminated the complex nature of caregiving relationships and the subtle ways that personal or cultural biases impact both individuals in these interactions. For example, a respondent stated that the theatre experience served as "a reminder of how even small things can be perceived [as bias] when someone is already feeling vulnerable."

Although the vast majority of responses to the transformative theatre experience were positive, some audience members provided negative feedback, represented by the following comments,, "we are a nonbiased facility and we don't 'genderize' or base our activities on sexual orientation," and "we treat all our patients with respect, and treat everyone the same. I don't see why we need to keep talking about how we are different, rather than how we are alike." These comments raise concerns that perhaps the perception of some in the audience is that the older adults who are LGBT are asking for "special treatment," rather than care that is personally and culturally competent, as is expected for all older adults. Perhaps the intensity of the scripted piece was threatening to some of the audience members in that it challenges the notion that all older adults are the same and that basic respectful treatment is not enough if you aim to provide patient-centered health care. Although transformative theatre expects to engender empathy among audience members this feedback suggests that this response is not universal.

Limitations

This project's evaluation is limited in several ways. Although using a convenience sample allowed *Aggie's Story* to reach the desired target audience, those who completed the assessments were self-selected that may potentially bias the findings. The data collection instruments, although standardized, have not yet been validated, and the limited data collected does not allow for statistical testing. As such, findings may not be generalizable to broader audiences. Analyses indicate that the theatre experience may be an effective training tool. However, more robust research with a randomized control group, and follow-up surveys to determine if the training resulted in adopting practice changes should be undertaken to substantiate this preliminary evidence. This would minimize the potential for social desirability bias as participants may have been more likely to provide positive feedback because they wanted to make a good impression on the discussant.

Likewise, *Aggie's Story* is geared toward discussions about older adults who are LGBT in general and does not dig deeper into concerns that are specific to diverse subpopulations of adults who are LGBT that are defined by gender, race, ethnicity, and other identifying characteristics. The cast of *Aggies' Story* are all White, ranging in age from late twenties to early seventies, and two cast members are gay or lesbian. Script scenarios and casting might be qualitatively different if modified for specific audiences and result in different findings. Increasing sensitivity to the choice of actors, settings, and stories in future productions of *Aggie's Story* could increase its relevance to diverse audiences. Future research could attempt to examine the nuanced differences between multiple groups and how these differences might affect the health care encounter.

DISCUSSION

The lessons learned through the transformative theatre experience described here indicate that it is a promising method of engaging audiences to examine their biases, and move them toward provision of more inclusive, culturally competent care of older adults who are LGBT. In our experience, audiences of health professionals felt enriched by the experience and the vast majority signaled plans to integrate knowledge gained into their practices.

The use of theatre allowed the audience to engage with *Aggie's Story* as observer and participant. As an observer they were exposed to typical experiences in the lives of older adults and could see the effect that biased treatment had on the characters in the scripted piece. As a participant in the interactive dialogue audience members are given permission to ask questions of the story characters and get feedback from the characters about how it felt to be treated as they were. This experience was helpful in allowing the audience members to explore the impact of bias on an individual level. The opportunity to explore individual biases could potentially lead to attitude and subsequent practice change that enhances the care provided to older adults. For older adults who are LGBT a nonbiased provider can be the difference between living a life of quality and dignity versus one of fear and self-doubt. It is encouraging that many audience members planned to use what they learned via the theatre experience in their work; future research could be enhanced by following up with participants to understand whether, and how, they carried out this intention.

As we consider the future of *Aggie's Story*, we would like to develop additional scripts that showcase other common scenarios faced by older individuals who are LGBT. The breadth of experiences that we could focus on is extensive. Many more stories need to be told so that providers understand older adults who are LGBT and members of the LGBT community are empowered with knowledge about aging services. Our group often discussed the intersections of race, gender, and sexuality as formative for many older adults who are LGBT and our hope is that we can use the power of theatre to convey these experiences as well. In addition, we are considering the development of a more advanced presentation for audience members who have experienced *Aggie's Story* but would like to learn more. We believe that there is also room to create a version for administrators in senior living environments that targets the challenges and opportunities associated with an inclusive, welcoming, and affirming living environment for older adults who are LGBT.

The Supreme Court marriage equality decision was announced as this article was being written. Although this landmark decision will lead to regulations aimed at protecting the rights of legally married individuals who are LGBT, it does not represent the end of the struggle to ensure that all people are treated equally. Regardless of marital status, individuals who are LGBT still face the more subtle forms of bias addressed in *Aggie's Story* in many health care settings. Those who are single or who are in a relationship but choose not to marry may not be protected from discrimination when seeking care.

In conclusion, this project evolved from a concern about how older adults who are LGBT were not equipped with sufficient information regarding their care needs, as well as how they might be treated as they try to access care, to a community-informed educational experience aimed at professionals in aging as well as the LGBT community. Providing an engaging educational experience came about through the use of a transformative theatre presentation that enables participating health care providers, as well as students in the health professions, to recognize biased behavior and be empowered to take action to correct it. Continuing to present this transformative theatre piece before numerous health care providers, health care administrators, and students may, in the long term, improve the provision of health care and aging services to older adults who are LBGT. It may also enable older adults who are LGBT to better prepare themselves should the necessity of living in a health care facility arise in their future.

Although most communities and universities do not have an interactive theatre ensemble, elements of this project can be adapted for wider use. Individual scenarios could be read and discussed by groups of students, professionals, and/or LBGT community members. It is our hope that this case study can serve as a model for creative projects in many communities, as we bring about the behavioral and systemic changes needed to support people who are LGBT as they age.

REFERENCES

Boal, A. (1985). *Theatre of the oppressed*. New York, NY: Theatre Communications Group.

Boal, A. (1995). *The rainbow of desire: The Boal method of theatre and therapy*. New York, NY: Routledge.

Boal, A. (2002). *Games for actors and non-actors* (2nd ed.). New York, NY: Routledge.

Burgoyne, S., Placier, P., Taulbee, M., & Welch, S. (2008). Investigating interactive theatre as faculty development for diversity. *Theatre Topics*, *18*(2), 107–129. doi:10.1353/tt.0.0029

Byne, W. (2014). Forty years after the removal of homosexuality from the DSM: Well on the way but not there yet. *LGBT Health*, *1*(2), 67–69. doi:10.1089/lgbt.2014.1504

Centers for Disease Control and Prevention. (2015). *Lesbian, gay, bisexual, and transgender health*. Retrieved from http://www.cdc.gov/lgbthealth/

Christensen, M. C. (2013). Using theater of the oppressed to prevent sexual violence on college campuses. *Trauma, Violence, & Abuse*, *14*(4), 282–294. doi:10.1177/1524838013495983

Dill-Shackleford, K. E., Green, M. C., Scharrer, E., Wetterer, C., & Shackleford, L. E. (2015). Setting the stage for social change: Using live theater to dispel myths about intimate partner violence. *Journal of Health Communication*, *20*(8), 969–976. doi:10.1080/10810730.2015.1018622

Fredland, N. (2010). Nurturing healthy relationships through a community-based interactive theater program. *Journal of Community Health Nursing*, *27*(2), 107–118. doi:10.1080/07370011003705013

Fredriksen-Goldsen, K. I., Emlet, C. A., Kim, H.-J., Muraco, A., Erosheva, E. A., Goldsen, J., & Hoy-Ellis, C. P. (2013). The physical and mental health of lesbian, gay male, and bisexual (LGB) older adults: The role of key health indicators and risk and protective factors. *The Gerontologist*, *53*(4), 664–675. doi:10.1093/geront/gns123

Garnets, L., & Kimmel, D. C. (2003). *Psychological perspectives on lesbian, gay, and bisexual experiences* (Vol. 2). New York, NY: Columbia University Press.

Hughes, A., Harold, R., & Boyer, J. (2011). Awareness of LGBT aging issues among aging services network providers. *Journal of Gerontological Social Work*, *54*(7), 659–677. doi:10.1080/01634372.2011.585392

Institute of Medicine. (2011). *The health of lesbian, gay, bisexual, and transgender people: Building a foundation for better understanding*. Washington, DC: National Academies Press.

Kimmel, D. (2013). Lesbian, gay, bisexual, and transgender aging concerns. *Clinical Gerontologist*, *37*(1), 49–63. doi:10.1080/07317115.2014.847310

Kimmel, D. C., Hinrichs, K. L. M., & Fisher, L. D. (2015). Understanding lesbian, gay, bisexual, and transgender older adults. In P. A. Lichtenberg, B. T. Mast, B. D. Carpenter, & J. L. Wetherell (Eds.), *APA handbook of clinical geropsychology, Vol. 1: History and status of the field and perspectives on aging* (pp. 459–472). Washington, DC: American Psychological Association.

Leyva, V. L., Breshears, E. M., & Ringstad, R. (2014). Assessing the efficacy of LGBT cultural competency training for aging services providers in California's Central Valley. *Journal of Gerontological Social Work, 57*(2/4), 335–348. doi:10.1080/01634372.2013.872215

Meng, A. L., & Sullivan, J. (2011). Interactive theatre: An innovative conflict resolution teaching methodology. *Journal for Nurses in Staff Development, 27*(2), 65–68. doi:10.1097/NND.0b013e31820eee5b

Moone, R. P., Cagle, J. G., Croghan, C. F., & Smith, J. (2014). Working with LGBT older adults: An assessment of employee training practices, needs, and preferences of senior service organizations in Minnesota. *Journal of Gerontological Social Work, 57*(2/4), 322–334. doi:10.1080/01634372.2013.843630

National LGBT Health Education Center. (n.d). *National LBGT Health Education Center*. Retrieved from http://www.lgbthealtheducation.org/

Project Implicit. (2011). *Project Implicit*. Retrieved from https://implicit.harvard.edu/implicit/index.jsp

Rogers, A., Rebbe, R., Gardella, C., Worlein, M., & Chamberlin, M. (2013). Older LGBT adult training panels: An opportunity to educate about issues faced by the older LGBT community. *Journal of Gerontological Social Work, 56*(7), 580–595. doi:10.1080/01634372.2013.811710

Salam, T., Collins, M., & Baker, A. M. (2012). All the world's a stage: Integrating theatre and medicine for interprofessional team building in physician and nurse residency programs. *The Ochsner Journal, 12*(4), 359–362.

Schaedler, M. T. (2010). Boal's Theater of the Oppressed and how to derail real-life tragedies with imagination. *New Directions for Youth Development, 2010*(125), 141–151. doi:10.1002/yd.344

Skye, E. P., Wagenschutz, H., Steiger, J. A., & Kumagai, A. K. (2014). Use of interactive theater and role play to develop medical students' skills in breaking bad news. *Journal of Cancer Education, 29*(4), 704–708. doi:10.1007/s13187-014-0641-y

Stein, G., Sherman, P., & Beckerman, N. (2010). Lesbian and gay elders and long-term care: Identifying the unique psychosocial perspectives and challenges. *Journal of Gerontological Social Work, 53*(5), 421–435. doi:10.1080/01634372.2010.496478

U. S. Department of Health and Human Services. (2015). *Lesbian, gay, bisexual, and transgender health | Healthy people 2020*. Retrieved from http://www.healthypeople.gov/2020/topics-objectives/topic/lesbian-gay-bisexual-and-transgender-health

Ward, B. W., Dahlhamer, J. M., Galinsky, A. M., & Joestl, S. S. (2014). *Sexual orientation and health among U.S. adults: National Health Interview Survey, 2013 national health statistics reports* (Vol. 77). Hyattsville, MD: National Center for Health Statistics.

Wernick, L. J., Kulick, A., & Woodford, M. R. (2014). How theater within a transformative organizing framework cultivates individual and collective empowerment among LGBTQQ youth. *Journal of Community Psychology, 42*(7), 838–853. doi:10.1002/jcop.21656

Yoshihama, M., & Tolman, R. M. (2015). Using interactive theater to create socioculturally relevant community-based intimate partner violence prevention. *American Journal of Community Psychology, 55*(1/2), 136–147. doi:10.1007/s10464-014-9700-0

Ageing, Drama, and Creativity: Translating Research Into Practice

JACKIE REYNOLDS, MIRIAM BERNARD

JILL REZZANO

MICHELLE RICKETT

Ageing, Drama, and Creativity was a pilot six-session interprofessional training course delivered collaboratively by Keele University and the New Vic Theatre, Newcastle-under-Lyme, as part of our Arts and Humanities Research Council (AHRC) funded Ages and Stages follow-on project. The course brought together a critical gerontological approach with arts-based educational practices and was designed to develop practice capabilities and age awareness among a diverse group of professionals working in arts organizations, the voluntary sector, local government, health and social services, and housing. This article describes how the course was developed and how participants were selected, details its aims and objectives, provides an overview of the sessions and a flavor of some of the exercises that were used, and considers findings from the structured evaluation alongside written reflections from participants.

INTRODUCTION

Developing gerontological interest in the humanities and in the possibilities of later-life creativity and personal change has sometimes been perceived as a slow process (Katz & Campbell, 2005). This can be linked to perceptions that view older people as maybe past being creative (Groombridge, 2006). Where research has suggested a decline in creativity in later life, this has clearly led to questions as to what extent such agist assumptions are self-fulfilling (Kastenbaum, 1992). However, though there remains a tendency for research agendas to be driven more by the problems of an aging population, there is also increasing recognition of the potential for personal growth and development through creativity and arts participation in later life.

Recognition of this potential, from a UK research context, was given a much-needed boost through the New Dynamics of Ageing (NDA) Programme: the largest research program on aging ever mounted in the UK (Walker, 2014). Funded by five UK Research Councils, the last phase of this nine year (2005–2014) multidisciplinary research initiative introduced a new focus on arts and aging by UK social gerontologists. It funded projects addressing a range of different art forms and types of participation, including studies relating to identity and the visual arts (Newman & Goulding, 2013); the impact of participation in music making (Hallam et al., 2011), and the role of arts and cultural activities in connecting older people in rural communities (Hennessy et al., 2013). The NDA also funded Ages and Stages: The Place of Theatre in Representations and Recollections of Ageing. This project (2009–2012) involved collaboration between Keele University and the New Vic Theatre, Newcastle-under-Lyme, Staffordshire, and was the impetus for the work we report on here.

Combining literary, cultural, and archival analyses with qualitative interview work and research-led practice, the Ages and Stages project undertaken by Bernard and colleagues (2015), provided theoretical and practical understandings of the role that theatre plays in the lives of older people and in the wider community. The research was drawn together to create a new hour-long documentary drama *Our Age, Our Stage* and the associated Ages and Stages Exhibition. At its conclusion, the project also received 12 months' "follow-on" funding from the UK's Arts and Humanities Research Council. The follow-on project, Translating Research into Practice, involved establishing the Ages and Stages Theatre Company, devising and touring a new performance piece, and scoping out the potential for a Creative Age Festival in North Staffordshire. It also included the development, delivery, and evaluation of the pilot training course we focus on in this article and which we titled Ageing, Drama and Creativity. The course intentionally brought together arts practitioners with professionals from health, social care, and housing backgrounds, and from the statutory, voluntary, and private sectors. Below we outline the origins and rationale for the course, describe the course content and how we incorporated theatre and drama into the sessions, and finally, from the evaluation findings, consider the implications for further educational work in this arena. We begin though with a brief review of some of the relevant literature and research to provide a context for what we have done.

A Growing Evidence Base?

Ages and Stages as a whole, and the training course specifically, needs to be viewed in the context of the limited existing literature focused on theatre and drama participation by older people and the ways in which it may be developed as a medium for the inclusion of older adults and young people. In 2014, two of the authors of this current article undertook a critical review for the Arts and Humanities Research Council's Cultural Value Project (Rickett & Bernard, 2014). Although the review drew on three earlier examinations of the impact of participatory arts on older people (Castora-Binkley, Noelker, Prohaska, & Satariano, 2010; Mental Health Foundation [MHF], 2011; Noice, Noice, & Kramer, 2014), it focused specifically on the cultural value that older people derive from their involvement in theatre and drama. The review included 77 documents consisting of published and unpublished research studies, evaluation reports, and descriptive overviews published as short pieces in journals, newspapers, and magazines.

The review highlights, in particular, the benefits and value of older people's theatre and drama participation on health and well-being, group relationships, and learning and creativity. In addition, a significant proportion of the literature focuses on the role of drama in enhancing or transforming group relationships, including through bringing generations together. One such educational example is a study by Hafford-Letchfield, Couchman, Webster, and Avery (2010), which discusses the process and evaluation of a UK intergenerational drama project exploring older people's sexuality. The project brought together social work degree students, an older people's theatre group, and three independent film makers and producers, to explore intimacy and sexuality in later life. The study not only challenged age-related stereotypes, but also highlighted the potential of arts-based research in informing practice, because it resulted in digital learning materials to be used in social work programs.

Other examples of educational activities exploring the use of drama in the context of older people's health and well-being include a study by Eaton (2015) who evaluated the feasibility of using ethnodrama—involving nursing students and residents in an assisted living facility—as an intervention to highlight late-life potential. There are also various examples of drama-based approaches within the training of dementia practitioners. Kontos, Mitchell, Mistry, and Ballon (2010) report on a 12-week drama-based educational intervention aimed at improving person-centered care. They assessed the effectiveness of the drama-based component of the intervention using qualitative methods and identified a range of positive outcomes. A similar focus and objectives can be found in the work of Anne Davis Basting, who specializes in creative engagement with people with memory loss. In 1996, Basting founded TimeSlips, an approach to creative storytelling, including staging plays that are inspired by people's stories (see Basting, 2003). Over the last decade, an extensive educational program has been developed to support the introduction of the TimeSlips program in a wide range of settings (TimeSlips, n.d.).

Other existing research echoes much of the early interest and evidence about the benefits of (intergenerational) arts participation more broadly, especially in terms of health and well-being. Pioneering work into health benefits was led by Gene Cohen, a U.S.-based psychiatrist, who published extensively on the subject of creativity and aging before his death in 2009. His research was concerned with understanding the physiological and psychological effects of arts participation on older people, and it was his work that importantly drew attention to the potential (as opposed to the problem) of aging in relation to creativity (Cohen, 2006), thus challenging a deficit model of later life.

In the United Kingdom, this orientation has been increasingly picked up by practitioners and funders of arts programs. Alongside the national NDA research program, the Baring Foundation was highly influential: launching a new funding program in 2009 to support arts organizations working in participative ways with older people. This program was initially informed by a report by David Cutler (2009), involving analysis of 120 case studies, which highlighted the value of arts participation for older people in relation to two inter-related dimensions of health (mental and physical), and to improved personal and community relations. However, the report concludes that despite the evident benefits, older people's arts participation tends to be overlooked in policy and service provision.

In further developing their focus on arts and aging, the Baring Foundation also commissioned the MHF (2011) to undertake an "Evidence Review of the Impact of Participatory Arts on Older People." The review included 31 studies and 2,040 participants and offers further evidence to suggest "that engaging with participatory art can improve the wellbeing of older people and mediate against the negative effects of becoming older'" (MHF, 2011, p. 4). Positive impacts in terms of mental and physical well-being were identified at individual, community and societal levels (see also Cutler, Kelly, & Silver, 2011).

Alongside these kinds of findings, there is also growing evidence of the benefits of intergenerational working—in cultural arenas as well as in welfare settings. Some of the benefits have been identified as "increased understanding, friendship, enjoyment and confidence," whereas outcomes specifically for older people have again been "related to health and wellbeing, reduced isolation and a renewed sense of worth" (Springate, Atkinson, & Martin, 2008, p. v).

Overall, the findings of existing literature, including the New Dynamics of Ageing program, broadly resonate with those of our own Ages and Stages projects (Bernard et al., 2015) and have underpinned our curriculum development activities. These findings include:

- The importance of challenging stereotypes that creativity declines/ceases in old age.
- The significance of excitement, challenge, and broadening horizons in terms of older people's theatre involvement.
- Connections between identity, belonging, well-being, and self-confidence and how they can be enhanced through theatre/drama.
- The importance of participation, volunteering, and taking part in creative activities, particularly at times of transition in later life.
- The potential of theatre/drama as a medium for the inclusion of older and younger people, for positive health outcomes, and community cohesion.

Alongside considering the implications of such findings and how to translate them into a training course, we also reviewed existing training opportunities to avoid duplicating current provision and to address unmet need. In addition, we sought to build upon our own extensive experiences (and those of colleagues) in delivering gerontological and drama-based training.

EXISTING TRAINING OPPORTUNITIES: IDENTIFYING GAPS AND BUILDING ON EXPERIENCE

It is pertinent to note that, in the United Kingdom, existing intergenerational training programs are often aimed at arts practitioners. London-based Magic Me, for example, is the UK's leading provider of intergenerational arts projects, and offers bespoke training for practitioners (Magic Me, n.d.). The Beth Johnson Foundation, a national charity sited in Stoke-on-Trent, hosts the Centre for Intergenerational Practice (Beth Johnson Foundation, n.d.). It too provides training for a wide range of organizations but, though it provides toolkits, guides, and other resources, these are focused mainly on the practicalities, funding, and structural aspects of intergenerational practice rather than on the use of creative arts-based approaches. In addition, a number of Higher Education Institutions in the United Kingdom and elsewhere have long offered a wide range of courses for those with an interest in gerontology. The Association for Gerontology in Higher Education (AGHE, 2015) produces an Online Directory of Educational Programmes in Gerontology and Geriatrics, which is a valuable source of information, especially for those studying in the United States. However, very few—if any—courses have a major focus on, or contributions from, the arts and humanities in general, or theatre and drama in particular, though they may address topics such as intergenerational relationships and late life creativity.

Some members of our research team have run academic programs in gerontology for more than 20 years (see, e.g., Bernard, 1995; Bernard, Bornat, & Johnson, 1999), and we have all been involved in the training of practitioners and professionals including social workers, teachers, psychologists, doctors, nurses and arts practitioners. We were therefore able to draw on these varied experiences, and on the work of other Keele University colleagues who, in recent years, have developed and delivered interdisciplinary short courses on aging, and on dementia, for practitioners in statutory and voluntary sector organizations (Ray & Chandler, 2012; Revell & Stockwell, 2013).

With backgrounds in drama, education, and social gerontology, the research team perceived a strong rationale for a training course that addressed gaps in existing provision and would bring together participants from different employment sectors and backgrounds to share expertise and experiences in relation to aging and intergenerational drama. Our own experiences and research had revealed the distinct lack of what might be termed a "critical gerontological sensibility" in much training-related and educational activity: rarely are arts practitioners and care professionals brought together in creative ways unless it has to do with addressing identified problems such as truancy or family breakdown. By contrast, the pilot Ageing, Drama and Creativity course originated in a non-problem-based and critical perspective and was aimed at those who wished to learn about the experience of aging and how to use creative drama-based intergenerational interventions.

The nonaccredited nature of the course meant that formal entry requirements were not necessary, and the fact that there was also no cost meant that we could aim to be as inclusive as possible. The pilot course was therefore intentionally wide ranging, aiming to offer insights and opportunities for reflection on critical gerontological perspectives, as well as practical tools and techniques for developing drama-based intergenerational practices.

METHOD

The Training Course

The course took place at the New Vic Theatre, Newcastle-under-Lyme, between February and April 2013. It comprised six 3-hour participatory workshops (see Table 1) that, as noted earlier, drew on the research we had done on the Ages and Stages project; on the various gerontology (Bernard) and drama (Rezzano) courses and training we had devised and taught for many years, and on the Ageing Studies Certificate being run by a Keele colleague for local authority staff. The workshops were facilitated by Dr. Jill Rezzano (Head of Education), with support from Dr. Miriam Bernard (Professor of Social Gerontology at Keele University). Formative evaluation of the course was undertaken by Dr. Michelle Rickett (Research Associate on Ages and Stages) who took contemporaneous ethnographic notes of what happened in each session and by Dr. Jackie Reynolds, who ran a formal summative evaluation session at the very end. The evaluation of the course received ethical approval by the University Ethical Review Panel at Keele University in September 2012.

Course Participants

Our intention was to pilot the course with 12 participants, but we received an unexpectedly high volume of applications and eventually awarded places to 18 of the 59 applicants. In selecting participants, the main priorities were to bring together professionals from diverse settings, and to select people who had specifically indicated how they might use the training within their own practice.

The 18 participants were drawn from: arts organizations, the voluntary sector, local government, health and social services, and housing. Freelancers and volunteers were included as well as paid professionals from organizations. The group included a wide range of ages (from 20–72) and career levels. Three were males and the rest female. They came from across a wide geographical area, including Stoke-on-Trent, Newcastle-under-Lyme, Staffordshire Moorlands, Manchester, Chester, Poynton, Wolverhampton, and Herefordshire. Although a number of the participants were experienced in working with young people, older people, or drama, they were all inexperienced in using intergenerational drama within their practice.

Curriculum Design and Development

As outlined in our literature review, the Ageing, Drama and Creativity course was informed by existing literature and, in particular, by the findings of the Ages and Stages research project. Those key findings, along with the gaps in existing provision that we identified were translated into the following overall aims of the course:

- To bring together professionals from a range of settings to learn and share expertise and experiences in relation to intergenerational drama;
- To increase the practice capabilities of learners by providing them with tools and techniques from drama, education and social gerontology;
- To increase the age awareness of learners through practical exercises, discussion, and reflection on their own experiences and professional settings; and
- To create a network of learners who would be able to continue to support each other and share their experiences after the training ends.

The variation of experience in participatory drama held by the group members necessitated an approach rooted in "active storytelling," common to theatre, and engaging members of the community in sharing and exploring experience (see also Schweitzer, 2007). This technique allowed for an accessible route to fulfilling our learning objectives and examining the key concepts and themes of the workshops. Verbatim quotes from the original Ages and Stages research interviews were used in a number of sessions as catalysts to making theatre, and also to prompt conversations examining the underlying assumptions behind the language we use about aging and older people. Our approach was also informed by the work of the Graeae Theatre Company (n. d.) who challenge the preconceptions and prejudices surrounding people (particularly artists) with disabilities, and who explore body image, similarity and difference, as aids to understanding. This work also resonates with Michael Mangan's (2013) recent exploration of the ways in which theatre represents aging and intergenerational relationships. Together, these approaches, with their examination and awareness of prevalent beliefs and the possibility of change, form the basis of much of our course and pedagogy.

Such approaches also require participants/learners to develop interactive physical and spoken responses, as opposed to being a passive audience. This was further built upon in the course through our use of Forum Theatre. Rooted in the practices of Brazilian Theatre Director Augusto Boal, Forum Theatre draws on the pedagogies theorized in his (Boal, 1979) work *Theatre of the Oppressed*. Participants are asked to show and dramatize incidents of oppression or prejudice from their life and to then invite interventions from other participants. These, in turn, are enacted in the drama, with the suggested remedies to the oppressive situation being a way of envisaging change. The objective is the empowerment of the oppressed individual through a community of support, which in turn strengthens community bonds and cohesion.

The course and its curriculum were thus underpinned by a combination of research, drama theory, and practice. The six workshops addressed key themes including aging, drama and creativity, stereotyping, intergenerational relationships, and intergenerational drama in practice, each addressing a number of the following learning objectives:

1. To introduce participants to thinking critically about aging and about how we socially construct older—and younger—people;
2. To explore how an understanding of the life course can inform experiences of aging and intergenerational relations;
3. To explore some key principles underpinning thinking about aging and the relations between the generations;
4. To examine myths and assumptions about aging, old people, and young people;
5. To examine the value of chronological age as a basis for understanding aging;
6. To look at the meaning of agism and examples of agism;

7. To look at how agism manifests itself in, for example, our workplaces and at how it can be challenged;
8. To look at how we can use this material and these experiences in creative ways to help challenge agism and inform other people's understandings of what aging is like—for both older and younger people; and
9. To provide opportunities for participants to draw on—and reflect upon—their own experiences in the workshop debates and discussions.

Participants were provided with a variety of academic and other resources in the form of articles, web links to podcasts and videos, and to organizations of interest. Three sessions involved invited speakers/performers, including members of the Ages and Stages Theatre Company, based at the New Vic. Halfway through the course, participants also attended a performance by the Company, titled "Happy Returns," at one of a number of regional venues (including care homes). Although there were no formal assessments associated with the course, everyone wrote a reflective piece about "Happy Returns," relating it to what they had learnt in the various sessions. In Table 1, we provide the outline of the course, identify learning objectives and resources for each session, and identify our relevant evaluation strategies across the course.

Evaluation Design

The research team adopted a qualitative strategy to the evaluation of the course, including the following methods and approaches:

- Contemporaneous ethnographic notes were taken by the research associate at each session.
- Participants were asked to write a reflective piece about their attendance at a "Happy Returns" performance. Eleven participants submitted their writing.
- A 45-minute evaluation session, led by Dr. Jackie Reynolds and Dr. Jill Rezzano, was included on the last day of the course. This incorporated a participatory tool (Body, Hearts and Minds tool; Buhaenko & Butler, 2004), which involves participants attaching post-it notes with written comments onto a large outline of a body, carrying a basket, and standing beside a bin: comments about things that they have learned or found interesting are placed on the head, things that they have enjoyed are placed on the heart, things that they have found useful for their practice and plan to take away from the course are put in the basket, and comments about aspects of the course that have not been useful, or they have not liked are put in the bin. The evaluation session also included a recorded semistructured discussion about participants' expectations and experiences, what

TABLE 1 Structure of Ageing, Drama and Creativity Course

Session Number	Description of Activities	Learning Objectives	Learning Resources/Activities/Evaluation Methods
1. Aging, Drama and Creativity: Introduction	• Ground rules exercise—Success indicators/hopes and fears • Ice-breakers—Various • Value line exercise • Lifeline exercise—Exploring participants' lifetime experiences • Decisions exercise—Conversations about decision making experiences, resulting in identifying key words and developing a drama based exercise • Introduction to issues around age and ageism, with a focus on personal reflection	1, 2, 3, 5	Selected readings on aging and age discrimination from Centre for Policy on Ageing; various research reports on aging and ageism Participants asked to collect age related/ageist images and information to bring to the next session Evaluation: Contemporaneous ethnographic notes
2. Aging and Stereotyping	A thematic workshop with practical exercises and examples focussing on images of aging, ageism and stereotypes • Ice breaker—Focused on identifying commonalities • Continuation of drama exercise that began in week 1, and discussing responses • Practical exercise exploring perceptions/assumptions; discussions translated into dramatic responses • Discussions of age related/ageist images that participants had brought in • A piece of forum theatre performed by Ages and Stages Theatre Company	4, 5, 6, 7	Various research articles on age discrimination; checklist of Essential Features of Age Friendly Cities (World Health Organization) For 'homework', participants were asked to complete a social network diagram, including ages and relative closeness of family, friends and colleagues over the life course Evaluation: Contemporaneous ethnographic notes

3. Understanding Intergenerational Relationships	A thematic workshop with practical exercises and examples exploring attitudes between the generations: • Warm-up exercise—'Name torpedoes' • Discussion based on age; 'How old are you and how old do you feel?' • An 'exercise in curiosity' based on New Vic production photographs. The photos were used as a stimulus for reading the relationships between people • Discussion about social network exercise, followed by a visualisation of one person's diagram • Discussion and practical exercise using Ages and Stages quote: exploring stereotypical assumptions • Guest speaker from the Beth Johnson Foundation; Discussions focused on intergenerational stereotypes and challenges of intergenerational practice	1, 2, 4, 5	Range of resources from Beth Johnson Foundation, including list of intergenerational resources; benefits of intergenerational practice; positive and negative stereotypes; stereotyping statements; planning for intergenerational practice, and practical exercises to encourage dialogue between people of different age groups Evaluation: Contemporaneous ethnographic notes
4. Happy Returns performances	By individual arrangement, all participants attended one of the Happy Returns tour performances by the 'Ages and Stages Theatre Company', and were asked to write a reflective piece about the experience	1, 3, 4, 5, 8, 9	Evaluation: Reflective journal entry

(*Continued*)

TABLE 1 Structure of Ageing, Drama and Creativity Course (*Continued*)

Session Number	Description of Activities	Learning Objectives	Learning Resources/Activities/Evaluation Methods
5. Intergenerational Practice, Drama and Creativity I	A task-oriented workshop giving participants the opportunity to focus on their own intergenerational practice or professional context • Warm up exercise—Letters and objects. Participants have 10 seconds to devise a visual image representing a letter of the alphabet • Improvisation exercise—Focused on global buildings/monuments • Local buildings—Further developing the theme of personal meanings attached to 'place': discussions of significant local buildings, based on photographs • Creating visual images of local buildings that could then be developed into a theatrical piece • Key exercise—An unidentified key is used to elicit memories and experiences that are translated into a theatrical piece	2, 4, 7	For 'homework', participants were asked to prepare a final course exercise. They were asked to devise a 10 minute practical exercise to show to the whole group in the final week Evaluation: Contemporaneous ethnographic notes
6. Intergenerational Practice, Drama and Creativity II	The focus for this final session was on participants applying their learning. The session included: • Warm-up exercises—Name memory games • Group presentations of 10-minute practical exercises that could be used in work settings • Course evaluation	2, 4, 6, 8, 9	Evaluation: Contemporaneous ethnographic notes Overall course evaluation: Incorporated a participatory evaluation exercise, semi-structured (recorded) group discussion and follow-up emails

worked well/less well, and how they would use the learning within their own settings. Ten participants took part in this session.
- Follow-up e-mails were sent out following the evaluation session, with the aim of including the views of those who were absent on that day, and also to capture any further reflections from those who had attended the session. Four e-mail responses were received, three of which were from participants who had attended the final session.

Thematic analysis (by hand) of the reflective writings, responses to the participatory tool, semistructured discussion, and e-mail responses was undertaken initially by Dr. Reynolds. Other members of the research team looked at the data independently, and themes were then cross-checked in team discussions. Although there was general agreement regarding the themes, these discussions helped to refine the analysis. The ethnographic notes were used to create a detailed descriptive account of participant responses to the sessions; they have not been thematically analyzed but rather used to provide a narrative of particular aspects of the course.

We now turn out attention to the key evaluation findings, before concluding with our thoughts about the implications of our experiences for others and for our future practice.

EVALUATION FINDINGS

We present our evaluation findings in three sections, each of which is informed by particular analytic methods used. We begin by focusing on the "Happy Returns" performances, drawing upon the reflective journals that were submitted by course participants. We then focus on the practical exercises that students undertook in the final session of the course, by presenting evidence from the contemporaneous ethnographic notes made during this session. Finally, we present the findings of the final participatory evaluation session, following thematic analysis of the data that we collected.

Happy Returns Performances

"Happy Returns" is an interactive forum theatre piece, exploring intergenerational relationships, and set at a birthday party for three friends of different ages. The audience is included in a range of activities designed to generate reflection and discussion on issues of aging and intergenerational relationships.

One example of the ways in which the audience is engaged in the action is a scene focusing on an older character's fear when passing a small group of teenagers on the street at night. The fears and assumptions of the older character and the group of young people are voiced by the actors. They did not actually communicate directly with each other. The actors then ask audience members for their response to the scene and how they might have responded in a similar situation.

Course participants all attended a performance of "Happy Returns," and 11 of them submitted a reflective journal entry about the experience. Their reflective pieces focus on various themes, including the quality of the acting, the issues that the play addresses, and observations of audience engagement. The most significant aspects of the feedback in terms of this article are the ways in which attending the performance supported the learning outcomes of the course and impacted on participants. For one participant, the performance had made her question stereotypes about aging, and encouraged her to return to studying the issues associated with this:

> The piece made me reflect on how much my own preferences and attitudes have changed with time, as well as making me question some of my own perceptions of age stereotypes. I think I may even return to some of the books about aging that I studied during my university days in order to ponder the questions that it raised further!

For another participant, the key thing was the opportunity to see the principles taught on the course applied in practice, which gave her ideas for how to do the same in her own practice:

> As the party got underway, I recognized elements of what we had covered in the workshops and the theory then had more reality as I connected it to the actual practice…. I will be considering these elements and how I can integrate them into my practice. I am considering a staff workshop so that I can pass on some of the exercises and they can then facilitate workshops with our customers.

Several other participants identified ways in which they could apply their learning in specific contexts, including a theatre education professional who learnt new approaches to developing drama projects with intergenerational groups:

> Overall, I was surprised by the piece as it was totally different to what I had expected. I think I was expecting a more traditional narrative approach as I would see in my own theatre venue. It has helped me to "think outside the box" in terms of forward planning for any future intergenerational drama projects.

Even for those with no background in theatre, the performance was seen as a valuable illustration of the potential of drama in the context of intergenerational practice:

> I think the performance is a useful addition to the New Vic Ageing, Drama & Creativity course content, showing what kind of projects can be mounted and how issues of age and aging can be explored, other than through academic research. It is a useful and important introduction for anyone who has never been involved in any form of issue-based arts development work.

Various comments, including the quote above, highlight the value of integrating the performance as part of the Ageing, Drama and Creativity course.

Practical Exercises

Ten participants took part in this final workshop, in which they were asked to demonstrate and apply their learning from the course by developing a 10-minute exercise that could be used in their work setting. This could either be based on an exercise covered in the course, or an original exercise. They were put into preallocated groups, according to their work area: housing/outreach, arts, health and social care, and voluntary/cultural sector. The following account of the session is based on contemporaneous ethnographic notes. On the day, the participants worked in groups of two and three and each group approached the task in a variety of ways, including:

- An exercise focused on place, which used photographs as the main stimulus;
- An exercise that explored and challenged generational perceptions and stereotypes, using photographs initially and, later, toys and literature;
- An exercise focused on holidays and sensory memories, using postcards as the initial stimulus; and
- An exercise using drama that explored stereotypical assumptions between people of different generations.

Our use of visual provocations throughout the course reflected a classically theatrical approach to devising work and this was clearly influential in the exercises designed and delivered by participants. Three out of the four groups used graphic stimuli, including photographs and postcards. The fourth used a dramatic scene between an older and younger person to focus on assumptions and stereotypes and used changing audience perspectives to reveal the actuality of the encounter.

As a nonaccredited, pilot training course, formal grading was not used, but rather verbal feedback from the workshop leader. The main strengths of the activities included the choices of resources that were used effectively by participants to challenge stereotypes though developing visual narratives. This involved clearly evidenced collaboration between participants. There were some suggestions for improvement, such as attention to pace and ideas for follow-up activities, though these may have been addressed given more preparation and delivery time. As well as participants demonstrating their own learning, part of the value of the exercise lay in the opportunity to observe the approaches of others, and to give feedback, thus developing their critical skills.

Final Evaluation Session

The summative evaluation of the Ageing, Drama and Creativity course, together with email responses, reveals a range of positive outcomes for participants that we have grouped into the following themes: style of learning, understanding agism, impact on practice, networks, and suggestions for the future.

STYLE OF LEARNING

Participants provided various insights into what worked well, and there were numerous positive comments about the mix of activities and the delivery style. For example, "There was a good mix of active participation and the delivery of information. It encouraged us to be reflective learners, examining both our own practice and our beliefs about aging."

The new ideas that were generated were found by some participants to be refreshing and inspirational: "I just found doing this course so refreshing… And it's lovely to have that kind of energy back into my own practice and what I do." There were also several positive comments relating to people valuing the opportunity to see the "Happy Returns" intergenerational theatre piece as part of the course.

As noted earlier, in the final session of the course, participants worked in groups to develop and lead a short exercise that could be used with intergenerational groups. This was found to be a particularly valuable experience, in terms of leading the session, and as a result of the opportunity to learn from others. This was highlighted in the group discussion when comments included, "I loved facilitating the sessions at the end. Really allowed me to think of ways to put things into practice," and "Everyone's different take on final workshop exercises was fabulous and has given me loads of ideas."

UNDERSTANDING AGISM

Participants' age awareness appeared to improve through insights gained from the academic resources and inputs, and through reflecting on and sharing their own experiences. One participant commented that she had learned more about agism and that she now understood its prevalence; another noted that it "was wonderful to reflect on my own experience of ageing." Taking part in the course had led one participant to independently read more about aging and different people's experiences of it. Another participant reflected on the personal and professional impact of her increased understanding of age-related issues:

> The benefits are hard to quantify in a specific way but in general terms my awareness of what it is to age, the impact of prejudice towards the elderly, institutionalized agism and the portrayal of stereotypes have all been highlighted and these are points which will definitely influence the work I do. On a personal level, I am far more aware of not making agist assumptions or remarks; elderly people have become more visible to me in my day-to-day life and I make a conscious effort not to make assumptions based on age-related stereotypes.

Impact on Practice

An active learning approach, through which participants took part in a wide range of practical ice breakers, exercises, and games, gave people many ideas for activities that they could use in groups that they work with. Some reported increased confidence in facilitating activities, and some gave specific examples of how they had already adapted their own practice to include approaches/techniques learned on the course. One participant commented that, "I will take away the practical ideas. I have never facilitated drama sessions before; however, I am currently coordinating an intergenerational quilting project and lots of these exercises would complement this project."

Another discussed the ways in which she had used many of the activities in her creative writing workshops with children, and how her overall approach to developing workshops had been influenced by her realization of the links between different creative art forms:

> I've come to appreciate even more quite how closely arts activities relate to one another—art, drama, music and writing are all interlinked and impact upon each other in intriguing ways. This is something that's been a useful realization and I have found that I'm incorporating music, movement, improvisation and art into my workshops much more than I previously had.

For a number of other participants, attending the course had prompted them to plan new intergenerational projects—for example, "[I] Will look at setting up intergenerational projects for dyslexic students and mums." Furthermore, not all participants were experienced in working with older people and, for one person, the course had prompted her to reject the notion that she could only work with young people. There was some interest in further study, including a learner who was applying to study on a Developing Arts for

Health course, and there were also initial indications that some learning was being cascaded to work colleagues (though this would require a longer term evaluation strategy to fully assess). We do also acknowledge the possibility that the course may have affected more significantly those participants who completed the evaluations than those who did not. A longer term evaluation would be valuable in fully assessing longer term and unexpected outcomes, and also in identifying those for whom the course had limited impact on their practice.

NETWORKS

A particular strength of the course was the diverse ages and backgrounds of participants, which provided a range of different experiences and perspectives, as well as establishing networks to help develop future projects. People valued the opportunity to network with other professionals interested in using intergenerational drama in a range of settings and to draw from each other's experiences, ideas, and expertise. We know too that some participants have maintained contact with each other and indeed with us: some having become involved in subsequent local developments including the realization of plans to hold an annual festival celebrating creativity in later life and showcasing the work of older people, arts organizations and practitioners (Live Age Festival, n.d.).

SUGGESTIONS FOR THE FUTURE

One participant felt that the experience of leading the final workshop activity had been such a boost to her confidence that it would have been good to have had similar opportunities earlier in the course perhaps by contributing to leading warm-up or ice-breaking activities. There were also a number of other comments about what could be done differently in the future. Participant numbers had fluctuated, partly due to adverse winter weather conditions, and because not everyone could attend every session. A small number of participants suggested that this made it more difficult for the group to get to know each other though some people did stay on to have lunch together after some sessions. Setting aside time for networking at each session might help address this on any future course.

Although the practical nature of the course seemed to be very successful, one participant expressed further interest in the theoretical basis of the work, and in related research. A future course could potentially include more academic content, depending on levels of interest. Similarly, a more wide-ranging and challenging reading list could help those participants who wish to engage more deeply with theory. Finally, given more time, it may have been valuable to include a short evaluation exercise at the end of each workshop, to capture people's more immediate reflections.

CONCLUSIONS

In conclusion, the level of interest generated by the Ageing, Drama and Creativity course is an important finding in itself, demonstrating the potential demand for such arts-based interprofessional and interdisciplinary training. Moreover, the feedback from participants was overwhelmingly positive, with the approach to active learning, the opportunities for reflection on one's own attitudes and experiences of aging, and the emphasis on gaining ideas and tools to be applied in people's practice, all being seen as particularly valuable aspects of the course.

The course was also a valuable opportunity to further develop the impact of the original Ages and Stages project by using (some of) our research findings and practical drama/devising techniques to directly inform teaching and learning. We were thus able to draw together perspectives from critical gerontology with those from best practice in drama and theatre education, and to enrich them with original research data and findings. Our work thus builds upon the increasing interest in interdisciplinary collaborations, and arts-based research, and highlights ways in which innovative partnerships between academics and arts practitioners can result in programs of training that deepen impact and engagement in theory and practice. This approach sits comfortably, we would suggest, with developments over the last decade in what the American cultural commentator and literary critic Margaret Morganrothe Gullette (2004, 2008) terms "age studies." Age studies endeavors to understand age and aging as complex, intersectional, social, and psychological constructions, and as a set of mediated relationships among people located at different phases of the life course. Moreover, we would concur strongly with Gullette (2015, p. 27) when she also argues that it "should be something that the youngest can look forward to with anticipation."

Finally, in research terms, it would be instructive to follow-up participants and, educationally, it would be encouraging if the pilot course could be adopted, at least in part, alongside other continuing professional development opportunities in our own institution or elsewhere. It is, however, pertinent to note that as our population continues to age, many higher education institutions in the United Kingdom seem to be withdrawing from, rather than investing in, gerontological education.

ACKNOWLEDGMENTS

We wish to acknowledge the contributions and support of the participants on the course, the Ages and Stages Theatre Company, and colleagues at the New Vic Theatre and Keele University.

FUNDING

This article arises from one element of our work on the project titled Ages and Stages: Translating Research into Practice. It was funded from 2012-13 by the U.K.'s Arts and Humanities Research Council (AH/K000764/1).

REFERENCES

Association for Gerontology in Higher Education. (2015). *Online directory of educational programmes in gerontology and geriatrics*. Washington, DC: Author. Retrieved from http://www.aghedirectory.org/
Basting, A. (2003). Reading the story behind the story: Context and content in stories by people with dementia. *Generations, 27*(3), 25–29.
Bernard, M. (1995). Teaching gerontology: Reflections from a British university. *Education and Ageing, 10*(2), 90–102.
Bernard, M., Bornat, J., & Johnson, J. (1999). Social gerontology education: Is there a future? *Generations Review, 9*(3), 4–8.
Bernard, M., Rickett, M., Amigoni, D., Munro, L., Murray, M., & Rezzano, J. (2015). Ages and stages: The place of theatre in the lives of older people. *Ageing and Society, 35*(6), 1119–1145. doi:10.1017/S0144686X14000038
Beth Johnson Foundation. (n.d.). *Beth Johnson Foundation: A future for all ages*. Retrieved from https://www.bjf.org.uk/
Boal, A. (1979). *Theatre of the oppressed*. London, England: Pluto.
Buhaenko, H., & Butler, V. (2004). *What men and women want: A practical guide to gender and participation*. Oxford, England: Oxfam. Retrieved from http://policy-practice.oxfam.org.uk/publications/what-men-and-women-want-a-practical-guide-to-gender-and-participation-115407
Castora-Binkley, M., Noelker, L. S., Prohaska, T., & Satariano, W. (2010). Impact of arts participation on health outcomes for older adults. *Journal of Aging, Humanities, and the Arts, 4*(4), 352–367. doi:10.1080/19325614.2010.533396
Cohen, G. (2006). Research on creativity and aging: The positive impact of the arts on health and illness. *Generations, 30*(1), 7–15.
Cutler, D. (2009). *Ageing artfully: Older people and professional participatory arts in the UK*. London, England: Baring Foundation.
Cutler, D., Kelly, D., & Silver, S. (2011). *Creative homes: How the arts can contribute to quality of life in residential care*. London, England: Baring Foundation. Retrieved from http://www.baringfoundation.org.uk/CreativeCareHomes.pdf
Eaton, J. (2015). The feasibility of ethnodrama as intervention to highlight late life potential for nursing students and older adults. *Gerontology & Geriatrics Education, 36*(2), 204–222. doi:10.1080/02701960.2015.1015122
Graeae Theatre Company. (n d.). Retrieved from http://www.graeae.org
Groombridge, B. (2006). *Extra time: Arts, health and learning in later life: Frank Glendenning Memorial Lecture 2006* (summary document). Leicester, UK: NIACE (National Institute of Adult Continuing Education). Retrieved from http://www.cpa.org.uk/aea/Frank_Glendenning_Memorial_Lecture-2006.pdf

Gullette, M. M. (2004). *Aged by culture*. Chicago, IL: University of Chicago Press.

Gullette, M. M. (2008). What exactly has age got to do with it? My life in critical age studies. *Journal of Aging Studies, 22*(2), 189–195. doi:10.1016/j.jaging.2007.12.004

Gullette, M. M. (2015). Aged by culture. In J. Twigg & W. Martin (Eds.), *Routledge handbook of cultural gerontology* (pp. 21–28). Abingdon, England: Routledge.

Hafford-Letchfield, T., Couchman, W., Webster, M., & Avery, P. (2010). A drama project about older people's intimacy and sexuality. *Educational Gerontology, 36*(7), 604–621. doi:10.1080/03601270903324511

Hallam, S., Creech, A., Gaunt, H., Pincas, A., Varvarigou, M., & McQueen, H. (2011). *Music for life project: The role of participation in community music activities in promoting social engagement and well-being in older people* (NDA Findings 9) Sheffield, UK: NDA Research Programme. Retrieved from: http://www.newdynamics.group.shef.ac.uk/nda-findings-9.html

Hennessy, C., Jones, R., Phippen, A., Maramba, I., Giarchi, G., Lankshear, G., ... Fisher, R. (2013). *Grey and pleasant land? An interdisciplinary exploration of the connectivity of older people in rural civic society* (NDA Findings 30). Sheffield, UK: NDA Research programme. Retrieved from http://www.newdynamics.group.shef.ac.uk/nda-findings-30.html

Kastenbaum, R. (1992). The creative process: A life-span approach. In T. Cole, D. Van Tassel, & R. Kastenbaum (Eds.), *Handbook of the humanities and aging* (pp. 285–306). New York, NY: Springer Publishing Company.

Katz, S., & Campbell, E. (2005). Creativity across the life course? Titian, Michelangelo, and older artist narratives. In S. Katz (Ed.), *Cultural aging: Life course, lifestyle, and senior worlds* (pp. 101–118). Canada: Broadview Press.

Kontos, P. C., Mitchell, G. J., Mistry, B., & Ballon, B. (2010). Using drama to improve person-centred dementia care. *International Journal of Older People Nursing, 5*(2), 159–168. doi:10.1111/(ISSN)1748-3743

Live Age Festival. (n.d.). *Live Age Festival*. Retrieved from http://www.liveagefestival.co.uk

Magic Me. (n.d.). *Magic me*. Retrieved from http://magicme.co.uk/

Mangan, M. (2013). *Staging ageing: Theatre, performance and the narrative of decline*. Bristol, UK: Intellect.

Mental Health Foundation. (2011). *An evidence review of the impact of participatory arts on older people*. Edinburgh, UK: Author.

Newman, A., & Goulding, A. (2013). *Contemporary visual art and identity construction—Well-being among older people* (NDA Findings 26). Sheffield, UK: NDA Research Programme. Retrieved from http://www.newdynamics.group.shef.ac.uk/nda-findings-26.html

Noice, T., Noice, H., & Kramer, A. (2014). Participatory arts for older adults: A review of benefits and challenges. *The Gerontologist, 54*(5), 741–753. doi:10.1093/geront/gnt138

Ray, M., & Chandler, S. (2012). Ageing studies certificate: Information for local authorities. (Unpublished report). Newcastle-under-Lyme, UK: Keele University.

Revell, A., & Stockwell, S. (2013). Ageing studies certificate: Evaluation report. (Unpublished evaluation report). Newcastle-under-Lyme, UK: Keele University.

Rickett, M., & Bernard, M. (2014). *Ageing, drama and creativity: A critical review* (Final report to AHRC). Newcastle-under-Lyme, UK: Keele University. Retrieved from http://www.keele.ac.uk/csg/research/ageingdramaandcreativity/Rickett_-Bernard.pdf

Schweitzer, P. (2007). *Reminiscence theatre: Making theatre from memories*. London, England: Jessica Kingsley.

Springate, I., Atkinson, M., & Martin, K. (2008). *Intergenerational practice: A review of the literature* (LGA Research Report F/SR262). Slough, UK: National Foundation for Educational Research (NFER).

TimeSlips. (n.d.). *TimeSlips: Creative storytelling*. Retrieved from http://www.timeslips.org/

Walker, A. (2014). Towards a new science of ageing. In A. Walker (Ed.), *The new science of ageing* (pp. 1–23). Bristol, UK: Policy Press.

Index

active storytelling 85–6
adult education *see* reminiscences in courses for older adults, written
age studies 97
Aging and the Arts (online course): development and implementation 45–62; active learning 52; assessments 47–52; community engagement 51–2, 59, 60; discussion 60; discussion board 51; evaluation 53–4; graduate projects 52; identification of course resources 53; method 46–54; objectives for course 47; peer review 51, 58–9; results 54–60; wiki presentations 47–51, 57–9
Ageing, Drama and Creativity course 79–97; evaluation design 87–91; evaluation findings 91–6; evidence base 81–3; existing training opportunities: identifying gaps and building on experience 83–4; learning objectives 86–7; method 84–91; networks 96; suggestions for the future 96
ageism 7, 12, 80, 86, 87, 94–5
Anderson, L. W. 47
Apol, L. 14
Armbruster, B. 14
autobiographical learning 29

Baring Foundation 82
Basting, A. 53, 82
Bendien, E. 29
Bernard, M. 80, 83, 84
bias and discrimination *see* health encounters and LGBT older adults: educational tool of transformative theatre
Black, P. 8
Bloom, B. 47
Boal, A. 66, 68, 71, 86
Body, Hearts and Minds tool 87
Boyer, J. M. 53
Brody, E. M. 10
Buhaenko, H. 87

bureaucracy, administrative and medical 5, 10, 11
Burgoyne, S. 66
Burke, K. 7
Byne, W. 65

carers 10, 20
Carr, D. 45, 53
Castora-Binkley, M. 81
Chandler, S. 29
Christensen, M. C. 66
Clark, J. S. 9
Clark, M. C. 29
Clowers, M. L. 14
Cohen, G. D. 45, 53, 82
Cole, T. R. 1, 6, 45, 53
community engagement: online course in Aging and the Arts 51–2, 59, 60
consent 6
continuity theory 17
Coser, L. A. 14
courses for older adults *see* reminiscences in courses for older adults, written
cultural diversity 42, 59, 74
Cutler, D. 82

De Medeiros, K. 10, 41
deficit model 45, 82
dementia 81, 84
depression 65
Dill-Shackleford, K. E. 67
disability 65, 86
discrimination and bias *see* health encounters and LGBT older adults: educational tool of transformative theatre
drama *see* theatre

Eaton, J. 81
Egan, K. 14
empathy 7, 8, 39, 66, 68, 74
expressive reading 14

family dynamics: teaching via novels 5, 10, 11
Fraser, K. D. 45, 53
Fredland, N. 67
Fredriksen-Goldsen, K. I. 65

Garnets, L. 65
Gattuso, S. 8
Gibson, F. 29
Gorman, M. 9
graduate class: teaching via a novel (*Kate Quinton's Days*) 5, 12, 13–14, 16, 18–19, 25–6; *see also* online course in Aging and the Arts: development and implementation
Graeae Theatre Company 86
Groombridge, B. 80
Gullette, M. M. 97

Hafford-Letchfield, T. 81
Hall, K. J. 14
Hallam, S. 80
Hanna, G. 45
Harvard's Project Implicit 71
health and arts participation 82, 83
health encounters and LGBT older adults: educational tool of transformative theatre 64–76; *Aggie's Story* 69–70; aims of project 67; discussion 75–6; dissemination 72; evaluation 72–3; findings and lessons learned 73–5; limitations 74–5; negative feedback 74; patient-centered health care 74; project development 67–9; public theatre to create social change 66; transforming theatre experience 70–1
Healy, J. 14
Hendershott, A. 14
Hennessy, C. 80
Housden, S. 27, 29
housing 17
Hughes, A. 66
Hutchinson, L. 15

identity 30, 41, 66, 80, 83
Implicit Association Test 71
interactive theatre: educational tool for improving health encounters with LGBT older adults 64–76
intergenerational relationships *see* Ageing, Drama and Creativity course
internet *see* online course in Aging and the Arts: development and implementation
interprofessional training: Ageing, Drama and Creativity course 79–97; *see also* health encounters and LGBT older adults: educational tool of transformative theatre 64–76

Jarrott, S. E. 7

Karasik, R. J. 7
Kastenbaum, R. 80
Kate Quinton's Days: teaching via a novel 4–21; classroom use of novel 12; description of novel 9–10; discussion and conclusion 20–1; favored child/rejected child 10; goals 12–13; graduate class 5, 12, 13–14, 16, 18–19, 25–6; limitations and challenges 19–20; literature review: importance of integrating humanities and arts into gerontology and geriatrics 6–8; literature review: use of novels as pedagogical tool in gerontology classroom 8–9; memoir 10; pedagogical approach 11–12; reading aloud together (RAT) 14–15; realistic life 7; specific exercises 14–16; student reflections/observations 16–19; students and settings 12–14; terminology 12; undergraduate class 5, 12, 13, 14–18, 24–5
Katz, S. 80
Kenyon, G. 41
Kimmel, D. 65, 66
Kohl, S. 6
Kontos, P. C. 81–2

Lang, A. 10
Leyva, V. L. 66
LGBT older adults and health encounters: transformative theatre 64–76; *Aggie's Story* 69–70; aims of project 67; discussion 75–6; dissemination 72; evaluation 72–3; findings and lessons learned 73–5; limitations 74–5; negative feedback 74; patient-centered health care 74; project development 67–9; transforming theatre experience 70–1
life stories 10

McAdams, D. P. 28–9
Magic Me 83
Mangan, M. 86
mapping events and characters in novel 11, 12, 14–16, 24–5
memoir 10
memory loss 82
Meng, A. L. 67
Merriam, S. B. 29
Moody, H. R. 29
Moone, R. P. 66
moral capacities 6
Morgan, L. 8
Moss, W. G. 8

INDEX

narrative orientation, teaching with *see* reminiscences in courses for older adults, written

New Dynamics of Ageing (NDA) Programme 80

Newman, A. 80

Noice, T. 45, 81

novels, teaching via 4–21; administrative and medical bureaucracy 5, 10, 11; family dynamics 5, 10, 11; literature review 6–9; mapping events and characters 11, 12, 14–16, 24–5; memoirs 10; personal perspective of student 9; reading aloud together (RAT) 14–15; realistic life 7; terminology 12

Nussbaum, M. C. 6

online course in Aging and the Arts: development and implementation 45–62; active learning 52; assessments 47–52; community engagement 51–2, 59, 60; discussion 60; discussion board 51; evaluation 53–4; graduate projects 52; identification of course resources 53; method 46–54; objectives for course 47; peer review 51, 58–9; results 54–60; wiki presentations 47–51, 57–9

Oró, M. 6

Paige, D. D. 14

peer review 51, 58–9

Perlstein, S. 53

Polkinghorne, D. E. 28

Port, C. 5

Posner, R. S. 7

Powell, J. P. 28

Pratt, J. R. 16, 26

professionals: Ageing, Drama and Creativity course 79–97; *see also* health encounters and LGBT older adults: educational tool of transformative theatre 64–76

prosody 14

Puentes, W. J. 29

Randall, W. L. 27, 28, 29, 31, 39, 41, 42

Rasinski, T. V. 14

Ray, M. 84

reading aloud together (RAT) 14–15

reminiscences in courses for older adults, written 27–43; application in courses 34–40; authenticity 40, 42; content analysis 31–3; description of course: context and data collection 30–1; discourse analysis 33–4; discussion and conclusions 40–3; each day provides us with new memories 40; possible negative consequences 39; procedure 31–4; reevaluative character of reconstructed memories 30; teaching with narrative orientation 28–9; thematic and stylistic connections 34

respect 39, 74

Revell, A. 84

Rickett, M. 81

Rogers, A. 66

Rosenblatt, L. M. 8, 9, 15, 19

Rossiter, M. 28

Rubin, R. J. 7–8

Salam, T. 67

Saldaña, J. 54

Salinger, J. D. 5

Schaedler, M. T. 66

Schwarz, G. 9

Schweitzer, P. 86

self-awareness and self-understanding: novels 8–9

self-reflection and transformation: theatre 66

self-reflective learning/sense making *see* reminiscences in courses for older adults, written

sexuality 81

Sheehan, Susan: *Kate Quinton's Days* 4–21

Sheets, D. J. 6

sibling rivalry 10

Skye, E. P. 67

social construction 86

Springate, I. 82

Stein, G. 66

stereotypes 8, 81, 83, 86, 92, 93–4, 95

substance abuse 65

Sullivan, T. A. 14

Taylor, E. W. 28

Taylor, S. 33

teaching with narrative orientation *see* reminiscences in courses for older adults, written

terminology: teaching via novels 12

theatre: Ageing, Drama and Creativity course 79–97; transformative theatre: educational tool for improving health encounters with LGBT older adults 64–76

Tice, C. J. 8

TimeSlips 82

Toman, M. 7

training, interprofessional: Ageing, Drama and Creativity course 79–97; *see also* health encounters and LGBT older adults: educational tool of transformative theatre 64–76 undergraduate class: teaching via a novel (*Kate Quinton's Days*) 5, 12, 13, 14–18, 24–5; *see also* online course in Aging and the Arts: development and implementation

Walker, A. 80
Ward, B. W. 65
Waxman, B. 7, 8, 21
Webster, J. D. 29
well-being 82, 83

Wernick, L. J. 67
West, R. 6, 20
Westerhof, G. J. 29
Wiggins, G. 47
Wolf, M. A. 8, 9, 29
written reminiscences *see* reminiscences in courses for older adults, written

Yoshihama, M. 67

Zeilig, H. 6